D0609396

M.I. GLINKA

his life and times

A. Rosanov

Paganiniana Publications, Inc.
211 West Sylvania Avenue, Neptune City, N.J. 07753

M.I. Glinka: His Life and Times by A. Rosanov was originally published in the Russian language in 1983 by "Muzika" Publishers. Through the courtesy of VAAP, Moscow, this 1988 edition has been prepared by Paganiniana Publications, Inc.

Published by **PAGANINIANA PUBLICATIONS, INC.**
211 West Sylvania Avenue
Neptune City, New Jersey 07753

CONTENTS

4

Chapter 1
M.I. GLINKA

The name of Mikhail Ivanovich Glinka can be found among the names of truly great composers who constitute the glory and pride of Russian music. He was the first to express the Russian peoples' heart in music profoundly and comprehensively. The beauty and artistic truth of his compositions finds as warm a response in our hearts as it did in the hearts of Glinka's contemporaries. His music is both a national resource and an invaluable contribution to the treasure-house of world musical culture.

V.F. Odoyevsky, a Russian music scholar and critic, considered Glinka's music "a new element in the art", very artistic and original. According to Odoyevsky's apt remark, the great significance of Glinka's work lies in the fact that he opened "the period of Russian music", clearly differentiating it into two stages — a pre-Glinka stage and a post-Glinka stage.

Being a really advanced artist, Glinka realized in his work the best traditions of the Russian and West-European musical past. Glinka contributed a new page to the history of Russian music, lending an attentive ear to the breath "of today." He "...didn't stop his search till he found his own way necessary for Russian opera, Russian symphonism" (F.N. Livanova). Russian romance and Russian chamber music can be added to these areas.

The foundation of Russian classical music and the national classical music school is based on the same principles that made Glinka's music so highly artistic and his work a significant part of Russian culture in the first half of the 19th century.

A lively and sympathetic interest of the contemporary intelligentsia in folk traditions influenced Glinka's esthetic and social views; that was the basis of his mastership and originality. He formulated his ideas in remarkable words: "People create music and we, artists, only arrange it." In other words as Serov, a prominent Russian music critic wrote, "Music, as any other language, must be inseparable from people, from the soil of this people, from their historic development..." And it was on the basis of the development and original realization of various phenomena of a century-old Russian music culture, both professional and popular, that Glinka's art emerged.

His creative style combines, first of all, originally mastered elements of peasant folk music: vocal, solo and choral, and instrumental; its modal peculiarities, characteristic features of melody, harmony, formation and coloring.

FACING PAGE:
Mikhail Ivanovich Glinka (1804-1857).

An artistic penetration into the nature of folk music and intuitive ability to capture its national peculiarities are some of the remarkable features of Glinka's genius. Stasov, a famous Russian critic wrote: "Glinka was able to express purely people's spirit, thanks to an ability to descend to the depths of the truth and beauty…to draw its real features". Stasov's words emphasize Glinka's realization and appreciation of national culture and the cultures of other West European countries — Italy, Spain, Poland and also Oriental music.

Phenomena of Russian music in the 18th and the beginning of the 19th century affected Glinka's style too. As Levashova, a Soviet scholar rightly puts it, "Russian monumental choral style a cappella and Russian early opera and song-romance and folk-song tradition in the genres of the 18th century instrumental music influenced Glinka's art. Of course Glinka combined all these elements into a new quality of more perfect classical style. He was the first who managed to give wide scope, strength of idea, content and harmony of artistic forms to Russian professional music."

The captivating beauty and refinement of a flexible Italian cantilena he heard during his first trip abroad also had an effect on the formation of Glinka's melodies. But primarily it is the Russian national melos, principles of multiform music and the speech of the Russian people with which the composer's melodies are linked. It is so close to them that it was often considered by listeners, especially by his contemporaries, to be purely folk music.

Industriously, Glinka worked out his unusually "melodious" style which became the basis of the "music language" of following generations of Russian composers. This style meets the demands of professional mastery of composition, the strict rules of harmony and counterpoint. The great musician worked on polishing the technical side of it until the end of his life. He was searching for the reasonable combination of feeling and form — the harmonic junction of the main idea and its realization.

From his childhood, Glinka was brought up on the music of Haydn, Mozart and especially Beethoven. Later he appreciated *The Well-tempered Clavier* by J.S. Bach, oratorios by Handel, operas by Gluck. Glinka studied their compositions critically, paying special attention to the places which interested him as an artist. However, being classical in character, Glinka's music belongs to the new historic epoch, the period of the flourishing of romanticism.

Glinka's creative work progressed from "classic" romanticism to realism — a harmonious, psychologically true depiction of the world of human feelings and emotional experiences, the poetic representation of real life. His symphonism, closely connected with Russian folk music, is also inspired by its images. The musical drama of his operas, always subordinate to the main idea of the composition, is based on the development of conflicts or contrasting comparison of the main themes. In the opinion of O.E. Levashova, Glinka "gave Russian music a wide scope, led it to symphonic forms. Russian music of the early 19th century lacked this width of scope of music development, harmony and maturity of musical composition."

The composer's stay in Italy in the early 1830's proved to be very important for the formation of his ideas about the tasks of operatic art.

Program of a memorial concert given upon the unveiling of the monument to M.I. Glinka, 1885.

"Kamarinskaya." Fantasy for the orchestra on two Russian folk songs. "The whole Russian symphony school is in Kamarinskaya," wrote P.I. Tchaikovsky, "just like the whole of the oak tree is in acorns! And for a long time to come Russian authors will draw from that marvelous spring, as it will take a lot of time and effort to exhaust its entire wealth."

Having met Italian artistic intelligentsia interested in the liberation struggle against Austrian despotism as well as in artistic problems, Glinka came into contact with a new art in Italy — a mirror of his advanced ideas. That's why the acquaintance with modern Italian opera was of great significance for the young composer. The variety of its themes, now heroic, now colored with romantic melodrama, now realistic and true to life, its melodic treasure in which echoes of Italian folk songs and dancing rhythms can be heard — made an unforgettable impression on Glinka.

Judging by his letter to one of his friends, it was in those years that, under the influence of all the factors mentioned above, he began to think about composing a Russian national opera, on a subject close to the heart of the Russian people. He thought about his opera for a long time. *Ivan Susanin*, the first Russian classic opera, was the result of his artistic meditations. The composer was inspired by the legendary story of the heroic deed of a peasant from Kostroma who sacrificed his life for the sake of his Motherland. The story was suggested to him by the poet V.A. Zhukovsky. On this basis he created a grandiose opera-épopee, in which the tragic fate of Ivan Susanin personified the idea of the greatness of true patriotism. In his first opera Glinka formed the basis of the development of the Russian peoples' historical musical drama.

Glinka's principles of operatic drama were a good basis for a further development of Russian historic opera in the work of Mussorgsky, Borodin, Tchaikovsky and Rimsky-Korsakov up to Prokofiev.

Glinka composed his second opera *Ruslan and Ludmila*, a composition no less monumental than *Ivan Susanin* — on the subject of a fantastic poem, a folk fairy tale by Pushkin. The opera brilliantly presents love for the Motherland, an optimistic belief in a final victory of good over evil and light over darkness. The musically epic figures of the hero Ruslan, the legendary governor Kiev Svetosar, the coward Farlaf, the lyrical images of women, Ludmila and Gorislava are boldly drawn. Epic pictures of ancient Russian life are painted with a full brush together with colorful oriental scenes. Charming southern beauty and bellicose intonations found their echo in the compositions of a new Russian school's composers — a "Mighty Heap."

Having created the classical samples of Russian opera, Glinka in accordance with his position, also gave Russian art classical orchestral compositions which chiefly determined a further development of symphonism in Russia. The whole Russian symphony school is in *Kamarinskaya* — Tchaikovsky wrote. It was constructed on a remarkable modification of two contrastingly "linked" (as Glinka himself put it) Russian folk songs — a long, thoughtful wedding song and a vivacious dance song orchestrated with sparkling wit. Like national instrumental music, it became the ancestor of the scherzo (joking) genre in Russian symphonic music.

National folk songs and dances were the basis of both Spanish overtures — the brilliant capriccio *Jota Aragonese* and *Souvenir d'une nuit d'été à Madrid* — a poetic picture of a Southern night.

The composer had other aims while working at his earliest symphonic composition. The romanticism and elegiac refinement of the composition are related to Pushkin's lyric poetry: a line can be drawn from it to Tchaikovsky's waltzes and further to waltzes on Pushkin's poems and *Natasha's Waltz* in *War and Peace* by Prokofiev.

New principles of symphonic development of music material, understanding instrumentation as an element inseparable from the process of music composition itself, realization of the "beauty of orchestra" (as Glinka mentioned in his *Notes on Instrumentation*) expressive abilities of different orchestral sections and instruments, masterful techniques of composition, logic in vocalism, ability to reach that clear sound which is characteristic of Glinka's orchestra: all this makes it possible to consider Glinka the first great Russian symphonist and put his name in the first row of the world creators of symphonic music.

Glinka's remarkable compositions for piano and chamber-instrumental ensemble also make a significant contribution to his musical legacy.

There is a direct route from Field's singing refinement of Glinka's early romantic pianism (variations, nocturne *Razluka, Separation,* mazurkas, etc.) to piano works by Balakirev, Tchaikovsky, Liadov and other Russian composers. And his chamber-instrumental compositions such as *Trio pathétique* and brilliant *Big Sextet* became the ancestors of ensemble music by Tchaikovsky, Arensky, Rachmaninov and many other composers.

Glinka's vocal works in various genres are an invaluable contribution to Russian romance lyrics. He was the first Russian composer to successfully combine music and text as a whole poetic unity. In harmoniously refined form and including in itself a wide sphere of human feelings, it complements Pushkin's lyric poetry and it is appropriate that Glinka's best romances were composed on the poems of the great Russian poet.

His genius parallels that of Pushkin in 19th century Russian art. They were contemporaries and belonged to one and the same generation which gave birth to so many remarkable names in Russian art, Russian literature and Russian thought. They belonged to the young men who were close to the ideas of the Great French Revolution, who were spiritually formed during the years of struggle against the autocratic-serf rule turned into a strong movement which led to the Decembrists revolt.

Despite the differences in their natures, upbringing and fates, Pushkin and Glinka were freedom-loving products of their time who breathed its air and responded to the problems troubling them each in his own way.

Stasov wrote: "Glinka in many aspects has the same significance in Russian music as Pushkin has in Russian poetry. Both are great talents, both are fathers of new Russian arts — both are entirely national getting their great strength directly from their people, both created a new Russian language — one in poetry, the other in music."

Glinka's ideal of art as inspiration turning into a refined form as a reasonable balance of feeling and its expression is also close to Pushkin. Their works are full of light and optimism.

Artistically Glinka is many-sided. A great composer, he was also a prominent pianist, a chamber singer, a teacher of vocal art and fi-

Romance written to Pushkin's verse which is still very popular on the contemporary concert stage.

Alexander Pushkin, Russia's greatest poet (1799-1837).

nally a writer. Besides *Zapiski (Memoirs)* he also actively participated in the creation of librettos of his operas, and also left many samples of epistolary genre. He made a valuable contribution to each of these spheres of artistic activity.

It is astonishing how much he knew besides music, literature and painting. Glinka was interested in geography, zoology and botany. During his studies at the aristocratic boarding school, foreign languages were Glinka's favorite subjects. Besides Russian, by the end of his life, Glinka knew French, German, Italian, Spanish and Polish; he also studied English, Latin and Persian.

Glinka did not have good physical health but his spiritual health helped him to cope with all these numerous tasks. It was due to his spirit that he managed to overcome all the difficulties that he faced during the hard epoch of *Ruslan*. In the following years, besides several music compositions, he also wrote his wonderful *Zapiski (Memoirs)*. Hardships and illnesses affected Glinka's appearance only during the last years of his life, but they did not break his spirit or artistic aspirations.

As the greatest Soviet musicologist B.V. Asafiev wrote: "The personal life of the greatest, the most sincere master of Russian music was not particularly happy. Still more vividly is revealed his real life, his work as a struggle, as a heroic deed surrounded by indifference and contempt."

It was about the greatness of Glinka's creative work that Serov wrote in his obituary notice: "...if a composer by his melodic inventiveness, always new and original, and by his mastership of secrets in harmony, counterpoint and orchestration in his very first work is ranked with first class composers — if an artist in no way imitating, due to his great erudition, but rather instinctively, by his innate "high" musical talent — managed to approach some methods of the giant in music — Beethoven, — such an artist will undoubtedly be famous not only in his Fatherland but throughout the musical world...

The greater the talent of an artist — the more time it takes to appreciate him. But the time will come when the world's artistic community will realize the importance of the activity of this Russian artist and will realize how much he contributed to the sphere of musical thought by his brilliant achievements..."

Ludwig van Beethoven (1770-1827).

The great significance of Glinka's work for Russian and world music was recognized by some of the composer's discerning contemporaries. On the occasion of *Ruslan and Ludmila* Odoyevsky addressed Glinka's contemporaries in 1843 with such emotional words: "Oh, believe me. A luxuriant flower has grown on the Russian ground — it's your joy, your glory. Let the worms vainly try to climb its stem and destroy it — the worms will fall down and the flower will remain. Protect it, it's a tender flower and it blooms only once a century." Serov and Stasov considered Glinka "not an artist of the past but a great banner of Russian creative traditions in music." Livanova sounded still louder. Their musical creative activity, though they were very different, laid the foundation for further musical-analytical study of Glinka's heritage. They wrote his biography on the basis of their reminiscences of their personal acquaintance with the great composer.

Later the works by H.A. Laroche, his observations of Glinka's melodic peculiarities, in which Glinka combined "the main properties of Russian folk songs with elements of new life" and his harmony stemming from folk-singing, testified to his creative genius.

Hector Berlioz, famous French composer and music critic, highly appreciated Glinka's creative work too.

The influence of Glinka's music and his esthetic principles on the destiny of Russian music is invaluable. Being an inspired innovator, he bravely and originally outlined ways of its development for many decades.

Prominent Russian composers of the second half of the 19th and 20th centuries became in different measure "music descendants" of Glinka. Realistic creative work of Dargomyzhsky was formed under the influence of the artistic principles of Glinka of "the last period." Balakirev realized in his work many ideas inherited from Glinka and gave them to the composers of the "Mighty Heap." The touching folk character of Mussorgsky's compositions, the epic greatness of Borodin's music who devoted his opera *Knyaz Igor* (*Prince Igor*) to Glinka are close to him. "Glory to Glinka, who showed us the way of the truth," — M.P. Mussorgsky. His words are true for Rachmaninov's work and then for Prokofiev's. "Glinka created an entirely new school,... to the sphere of which I belong. I am Glinka's disciple," — P.I. Tchaikovsky wrote. "I am Glinka's follower," — N.A. Rimsky-Korsakov wrote about himself.

All this is the heritage of Soviet composers brought up on the high ethics of Glinka's ideas and musical images. Soviet composers developed and gave a new interpretation of monumentally epic and psychologically lyrical branches of Glinka's work, aimed at humanism and the creation of beauty for the sake of the spiritual benefit of mankind, full of a dignified sense of proportion and deep sincerity.

"The Soviet people love Glinka's music which has its roots in the Russian earth. His name is greatly respected both in our country and all over the world. The great son of Russia will forever be honored in his Motherland." A. Rosanov.

Third All-Union Vocal Competition, Moscow, USSR, named after Mikhail Glinka, The Great Hall of the Moscow Conservatory, 1965.

Watercolor portrait of M.I. Glinka by Y. Yakovlev.

Monument to M.I. Glinka in Smolensk
(sculptor A. fon Boch) erected on the initiative
and with the assistance of the composer's sister
and faithful friend Ludmila Shestakova.

Chapter 2
GREEN YEARS

There is a village called Novospasskoye a hundred miles from the ancient towers of provincial Smolensk on the deep Desna river. In this village the estate of Major Nickolay Alexeyevich Glinka was located.

Here at dawn on the beautiful spring morning of May 20, 1804 the second son was born to the family of Major Glinka's son, Captain Ivan Nickolayevich and his daughter-in-law Evgenia Andreevna. The boy was christened Mikhail. "His mother used to say that after the first cry of the newborn baby she could clearly hear the loud and melodious singing of a nightingale in the tree right under the window of her bedroom," — Ludmila Ivanovna Shestakova wrote afterwards about the birth of her brother.

For the parents who were still grieving over the loss of their first-born Alexei, the birth of the second son was a joy and consolation. Their position became still "more terrible," according to the words of Ludmila Ivanovna, when against their will they soon had to "hand over" the baby to the care of his grandmother, Feokla Alexandrovna. Later Glinka recollected that his grandmother had taken him to her rooms "...where it was very hot because of the stove that was lit though it was summer", dressed him in a squirrel fur-coat and treated him to sweet knot-shaped biscuits. A masterful old lady who was "not particularly kind" to her servants, enjoyed spoiling her grandson.

The six years that Glinka lived with his grandmother in suffocating conditions had a bad effect on his health. He caught cold easily. His mother spared no effort to get him used to fresh air but it was all in vain. It was only much later than Glinka became aware of the beauty of Russian nature.

The boy's life in his domestic prison was rather dull. It was one of the reasons why Russian songs and fairy-tales told by his nurses Tatiana Karpovna, Avdotia Ivanovna and especially Irina Feodorovna Meshkova made such a deep impression on him. When he was bored or ill his nurses used to humor him by singing him songs and telling him fairy-tales, the poetry of which touched little Mikhail. Russian songs were his favorite kind of music until the day he died.

To the joy of his family, the boy learned at an early age and liked to draw. He also adroitly imitated the ringing of bells: beating resonant copper basins he listened attentively to the sounds slowly dying away. Later he believed it was the first expression of his "talent for music." A purely national basis of his creative work was based on all these impressions that were imprinted on the heart of a future famous composer.

His grandmother died in 1810 and the management of the estate passed entirely to the hands of Ivan Nikolayevich Glinka. But hardly had he started his economic changes on the estate when the war of 1812 broke out. The burning patriotism of those years remained in the youthful heart of the future musician forever. Indelible recollections of the Russian people's greatness and heroism became the basis on which Glinka's personality as an artist and citizen subsequently formed and grew.

Feokla Alexandrovna Glinka (d. 1810), M. Glinka's grandmother, with whom he spent many years of his childhood. As the composer himself reminisced later, she was "a masterful old lady" who was not particularly kind to her servants but enjoyed spoiling her grandson.

The house in Novospasskoye, a village a hundred miles from the ancient towers of provincial Smolensk. Drawing by I. Vrangel.

"Capital of the North" with its huge well-proportioned buildings, squares and the Neva river made a deep impression on young Glinka.

The enemy rushing irrepressibly to Moscow through the roar of guns and blazing fires intruded into the Smolensk regino. "Captain Glinka with a large family on his hands went to other regions (goubernias)," — one of his contemporaries wrote later. I.N. Glinka with his wife and children settled in the city of Oriol for a while. Novospasskoye was not spared the attack of French marauders either; the country-seat was robbed in spite of the courageous resistance of the peasants.

Tumultuous days in Oriol where citizens greedily listened to rumors and news from the units that were fearlessly rushing to "the theatre of war" near Moscow didn't last long.

The remains of Napoleon's army that had seemed so formidable before had been crushed by the wise strategy of M.I. Koutouzov and were hurled back far from the borders of Russia. In spring 1813 the Glinkas returned to Smolenschina which still resounded to the echoes of its glorious military past.

The head of the family faced difficult tasks now. Guns were still roaring in the western part of Europe and blood was shed in a terrible "battle of peoples" near Leipzig. The Allied troops marched into Paris and peaceful life began again in Russia shattered by the war. I.N. Glinka had to think about the management of the estate and his children's upbringing as there were 13 children in the family by 1825.

First I.N. Glinka built a new house in Novospasskoye. L.I. Shestakova wrote that all the ceilings were painted and the walls of the main rooms were covered with velvet. "Furniture...made of a special kind of wood in every room. Splendid looking-glasses, parquets, chandeliers, lamps"; there were also two pianos. "A large sloping meadow stretched as far as the river...A large garden was covered with flowers, fountains, cascades, small islands...whimsical little bridges..." The family began to live "keeping up old traditions" and prospered.

A governess, Rosa Ivanovna, was employed for the children. An architect whose name is unknown was hired by Ivan Nikolayevich to teach Glinka to draw.

A good-natured "old man — a distant relative having noticed the boy's interest in his stories" about distant lands and savage people, about climates and works of tropical countries presented him with an edition of *History of travelling in general...* by A.F. Prevo d'Aksil, published by I.I. Novikov in 1782-1787. Little Glinka studied it "with passion" and made notes. He wrote in his *Memoirs* that it became the first basis of his "passion for geography and journeys". Being gentle and quiet by nature the boy preferred reading to children's games, but his feeling for music was still "undeveloped".

According to Glinka his feeling developed suddenly when he was 10 or 11. That was in 1814 or 1815.

On that day serf musicians of his uncle Afanasiy Andreyevitch from the village of Shmakovo who stayed in Novospasskoye after one of the family's festivities played a quartet with clarinet by Swedish composer Bernhard Krousel. His music made "an incomprehensibly new ravishing impression" on the boy. The next day he still felt something incredibly sweet. When the teacher asked him why he thought only of music, he replied, "There is nothing to be done, music is my soul."

Glinka's upbringing itself contributed to the development of his musical talent. He learned to read music while playing the piano with his "strict" governess V.F. Klammer and played the violin with one of his uncle's musicians. But a symphony orchestra remained for him "a source of the most lively ecstasy" — as Glinka wrote in his *Memoirs*. He also mentioned there that "sad and gentle" sounds of Russian songs, played with wooden wind instruments mostly at supper time, "might be...the first reason that I started working mainly at Russian folk music."

In autumn 1817 the news that the Ministry of Public Education backed by "the highest authorities" decided to organize an exclusive school at the Pedagogical Institute which was reorganized into a University two years later reached Novospasskoye. "A general education" received there was to provide the student with "access to scientific work" and above all to public service. Having thought everything over thoroughly Ivan Nikolayevich Glinka soon made up his mind. And in the middle of January 1817 his mother Evgenia Andreevna in "a comfortable closed sleigh" started for Petersburg together with her thirteen year old son Mikhail and her eldest daughter Pelagaya. On their way Glinka persuaded his sister that they, like Columbus, "were going to discover new lands and imagined himself Vasco da Gama"; he wasn't mistaken. A new important period of his

Wilhelm Kückelbecker, (1797-1846) Pushkin's friend in the Lyceum, poet and Decembrist, "a kind and noble man," Glinka's tutor.

The "exclusive school" at the Pedagogical Institute founded in Petersburg in the autumn of 1817.

ИСТОРІЯ
о
СТРАНСТВІЯХЪ
ВООБЩЕ
ПО ВСѢМЪ КРАЯМЪ ЗЕМНАГО КРУГА,
сочиненія
ГОСПОДИНА ПРЕВО,
сокращенная
новѣйшимъ расположеніемъ
Чрезъ Господина Ла-Гарпа
ЧЛЕНА
ФРАНЦУСКОЙ АКАДЕМІИ,
содержащая въ себѣ:
Достойнѣйшее примѣчанія, самое полезнѣйшее
и наилучшимъ доказанное образомъ, въ стра-
нахъ свѣта, до коихъ достигали Европейцы;
о нравахъ оныхъ жителей, о вѣрахъ, обыча-
яхъ, наукахъ, художествахъ, торговлѣ
и рукодѣліяхъ, съ пріобщеніемъ,
Землеописательныхъ чертежей и изо-
браженій вещей любопытныхъ.

Часть I.

На Россійскій языкъ переведена 1782 года
Дмитровскаго уѣзда въ селцѣ Михалевѣ.

ВЪ МОСКВѢ
ВЪ Университетской Типографіи у Н. Новикова
1–81 годѣ.

"History of Travelling in General" by A.F. Prevo d'Askil published in Russia in 1782-1787. One of Glinka's favorite books as a child.

life had begun. It was the end of his childhood and the beginning of his youth.

The view of the "Capital of the North" with its "huge well-proportioned buildings", squares and the Neva River "dressed in granite" made "a magic impression" on young Glinka. Later his father came. "Having learned everything, he got down to business" and the boy was put on the list of the boarding-school students on February 2, 1817.

Many of the children who then entered boarding school with Glinka became his life-long friends.

The course was to last four years. Three of them passed in a two-storied building on the bank of the Fontanka River near the eye-hospital of Doctor Gaye.

Not far from it rose the granite pavilions of Kalinkin Bridge behind which there stretched Kolomna — the quietest and poorest part of Petersburg. In accordance with his father's wish Glinka and three other pupils were accommodated in the attic of a house away from other pupils. In the garret attached to the attic the boy raised rabbits and pigeons which were his favorites and which felt quite at home there.

W.K. Kückelbecker, A.S. Pushkin's friend in the Lyceum, was appointed the boys' "special tutor." Glinka's schoolmate N.A. Marckevich, a future historian, described their tutor as "a kind and noble man." Wilhelm Kückelbecker taught Russian philology in the boarding-school. A man of high morals, a patriot, a future Decembrist he taught his pupils "to feel and think"; he tried to develop in their hearts a love for national history and literature and above all a love for Russian popular tales, "bylinas" (Russian epics) and songs.

In those tumultuous years, when Glinka's civic consciousness was developing, Kückelbecker's words undoubtedly made a deep impression on him. It might have been those very lessons that evoked in the future great musician his love for poetry, for the works by V.A. Zhukovsky, A.S. Pushkin, A.A. Delvig, I.I. Koslov.

Such teachers as K.I. Arsenev, A.P. Kounitsin, E.V. Raupakh were notable for their progressive views in the heterogeneous staff of the boarding school. According to Glinka they were people "of learning."

In his *Zapiski (Memoirs)* Glinka also writes about their "kind junior-inspector" I. Ja. Kolmakov who was a very "eccentric person." He calls I. Ja. Kolmakov "a consolation of the pupils" and says that his "funny tricks" often amused them. Afterwards the composer dedicated special works to him.

The nephews of Kückelbecker — Boris and Dmitry Glinka — lived in the attic of the boarding-school for some time. However they made friends not with their relatives but with Nickolay Melgunov, a future writer and music critic, and Sergey Sobolevsky. Pushkin's younger brother, Leovushka Pushkin, was also among the pupils of the boarding school.

Thanks to Kückelbecker and his friends who visited him the pupils came to know about the events of contemporary social and political life. It was significant that two of them, M.N. Glebov and S.M. Palitsin, took part in the Decembrist revolt on December 14, 1825.

It was at this point that Glinka met A.S. Pushkin for the first time. Coming to see his brother at boarding school he would go up-stairs to the attic to visit his "friend of school years," Kückelbecker. Poets Delvig and Baratinsky would drop by too. There they exchanged ideas and argued. Obviously Glinka sometimes might be present at such meetings.

Those were the years of the triumph of the Holy Alliance in Europe. The struggle of the autocratic régime against "a spirit of freedom" in Arakcheev Russia intensified. But at the same time a movement of popular protest and secret alliances of future Decembrists was growing. Public opinion was aroused. Trying to suppress it the régime took drastic measures which adversely affected the happy life of the aristocratic boarding school.

Kückelbecker was fired for reading poems devoted to exiled Pushkin. The Ministry of Public Education described the protest of the pupils almost as a riot. "Liberal", that is, progressive-minded professors, were discharged. A dull and bureaucratic atmosphere was established in the boarding school but the lessons continued.

Taking "a course of sciences" Glinka gave preference to foreign languages, including Latin and Persian, Geography and Zoology. Like Pushkin in his time, he was much less interested in Mathematics.

There was a piano in the attic which was soon replaced by a good grand piano made by I. Fischner, later taken to Novospasskoye. It is now kept in the museum of musical instruments in Leningrad. Glinka continued his lessons in music as soon as he came to Petersburg. John Field, a famous Irish pianist, gave him three lessons in playing the piano. Glinka met with his flattering approval. He learned and successfully played various compositions by J. Field. But Field soon left for Moscow. There were lessons with V. Oman, K.F. Tseyner and, at last, with Carl Meyer. Glinka thought that Meyer most of all contributed to the development of his "musical talent". Under his guidance Glinka became an outstanding pianist and later they became good friends. Glinka also learned to play the violin.

As Glinka recollected, his "parents, relatives and acquaintances" would take him to the theatre during his school years in Petersburg. The young man always "went into raptures" over the ballets and operas. He heard P. Zlov and V. Samoilov. Undoubtedly he also used to go to the theatre where famous Ekaterina Semenova acted in tragedies by V.A. Ozerov. He did not miss a chance to attend a concert and listen to the famous Petersburg serf symphony orchestra of P.I. Yushkov. At his uncle's, Glinka, together with his cousin Sofiya Ivanovna "pretty and fond of music and reading", played duets, usually overtures to operas, by Mozart, Méhul, Cherubini and Rossini. During his summer holidays in Novospasskoye he played music with K.F. Gempel, "a good musician" — a husband of his sisters' governess, listened to the "Shmakov" orchestra of his uncle Afanasy Andreevitch (which had "developed greatly" by that time) and sometimes even played the violin with the orchestra.

During the last months of his school life in spring 1812 Glinka, as he mentioned in his *Zapiski (Memoirs)*, composed variations on a theme of J. Weigl *The Swiss Family* "for a beautiful lady" with "pretty" silver soprano who played the harp very well. And soon af-

Anton Delvig (1798-1831), Russian poet, Pushkin's schoolmate and life long friend.

Evgeny Baratinsky (1800-1844), Russian poet. To his verses Glinka composed many a romance.

John Field (1782-1837), famous Irish pianist, composer, and pedagogue, whose flattering approval Glinka met in his young years.

Carl Meyer (1799-1862), pianist and composer who, according to Glinka, contributed most to the development of his musical talent.

ter that he composed variations on a theme by Mozart and a waltz for the piano. Those were his first attempts in composition.

On July 3, 1822 according to the magazine *Syn Otechestva* Mikhail Glinka played the piano concerto by Hummel. It happened on the third day of public examinations at the exclusive school of St. Petersburg University. Obviously he played the concerto so well that his uncle Afanasy Andreevitch took him to Hummel who "listened favorably" to the first solo.

Glinka was "the second on the list" i.e. one of the best students who graduated from the exclusive school. However he remained to start his public service. Though he didn't care for any of its branches, in particular, he studied German for some time as it came easily to him and was necessary for acceptance by the Foreign Board. But mainly he spent his time playing the piano and in composition.

The young composer's delicate health became worse as a result of his strenuous work.

In Spring 1823 his father wished to send his elder son to the Caucasus to recover. As Glinka wrote in his *Zapiski (Memoirs)*, doctors considered mineral waters useful for his scrofulous tendency. However the trip which was at that time a difficult thing wasn't that useful for his health but it enriched his receptive nature with many vivid and various impressions.

Glinka was entranced by white clay-walled cottages, apple-trees, cherry-trees in blossom, warm spring days and starlit nights in "the picturesque Ukraine" which replaced the "wet and fresh weather" in Novospasskoye which he had left with his former attendant Iliya and cook Afanasy. There came steppes covered with "aromatic grass" and at last the shining snowy peaks of the Caucasus appeared. Modern Pyatigorsk looked quite wild at that time; there were few houses, no churches and gardens.

"The majestic Caucasian mountain ridge was covered with snow...the Podcoumok river twisting across the plain and there were many eagles in a clear sky," Glinka recollected. "My friends and I settled in a small modest house. We were having a good time. One of us brought books, the food was all right...Soon we began to take the waters..." The grandiose beauty of mountain landscapes, depths of forests entangled with wild vines and vivid pictures of people's life remained in Glinka's heart forever. That was the first touch of the real East. "...I saw Circassian women dancing and Circassians playing and riding..." he wrote further in his *Zapiski (Memoirs)*. Such memories probably became the source of Glinka's inspiration in acts 3 and 4 of *Ruslan and Ludmila*.

But neither sulphur baths nor Narzan in Kislovodsk improved his health. At the end of August, 1824 Glinka started back to the North.

"Many new impressions inspired my imagination" — Glinka wrote in *Zapiski (Memoirs)*. Having returned from the Caucasus he started to work hard at music. Running his uncle's orchestra in whose repertoire there were symphonies by Haydn, Mozart, Beethoven, Méhul and also by Maurer, he studied methods of the classical composers and thus actually studied instrumentation. When in the village he listened to Russian folk songs. Perhaps many of them were familiar to him from his childhood. His creative work at that time is represented by *Andante Cantabile* (Adagio), two variations *Rondo* for orchestra and also by *Septet* for woodwind and string instruments.

Having returned to Petersburg in spring 1824 the young composer devoted his time to both the violin and the piano. Carl Meyer listened to him and said: "You are too talented to be given lessons; come to see me every day as a friend and we'll study music together." Nevertheless he continued asking Glinka to prepare "various pieces" and taught him composition.

Glinka was in no hurry "to start his public service" yet. However at last he was appointed an under-secretary in the office of the Ministry of Communications on May 7, 1824. Though he did not like the service, it made him more independent and left him enough time for music.

His portrait painted by M. Terebenev in water-colors that year apparently shows the originality of Glinka's youthful face. His face was sometimes "unattractive", sometimes "enthusiastic" with hazel attentive eyes able to "flash fire" at moments of inspiration. One can see the tuft on the right part of his head about which Glinka was so concerned in his early years.

Glinka composed the romance *Moya Arfa-My Harp*, the music probably related to his project of the opera *Matilda Rokby* by Walter Scott. He considered it "a failure" and called it *Before the Flood* as he wrote it before November 7, 1824, the day of a disastrous flood in Petersburg so brilliantly depicted by Pushkin in his poem *Medny Vsadnik*. Fortunately, the water, having reached the threshold of Glinka's flat, began to subside. Glinka composed his first "successful" romance only in the winter of 1825.

The same year, working "very hard", he composed his first string quartet, only part of which remains. He was also working at a sonata for viola and piano but he didn't finish it. However he believed that those compositions were "of great use," considering them exercises of a pupil.

Saint Petersburg. Outdoor fête on the islands. Drawing and lithograph by A. Brullov.

A Quartet written by M. Glinka in his youth. When in 1854 Glinka's friends played it for him, the composer . . . didn't recognize it.

20

Young Glinka gave a lot of time to "musical exercises" at the houses of his friends and acquaintances — the Siverses, the Bakhturins, the Gorgolies, the Demidovs. He took part in these parties both as a composer and as a singer since Beloly had given him several lessons in singing. He composed his first French quadrille for the parties in the house of Princess E.A. Khovanskaya. It was his first "public debut." But "when music started, couples began their movement, conversations started" and the music remained unnoticed. However, as P.A. Stepanov recollected, Glinka himself was satisfied and his friends were proud of him.

Zinaida Volkonskaya (1792-1862), brilliant amateur-singer and composer. Portrait by Carl Brullov, a celebrated Russian painter.

Praskovia Barteneva (1811-1872), an amateur singer. Portrait by Carl Brullov.

The tragic day of December 14, 1825 remained in Glinka's memory for the rest of his life. The time he had spent with Wilhelm Kückelbecker under the influence of his ideas and political views made a deep impression on him. On that terrible morning Glinka was present in Dvortzovaya Square and then in Senatskaya Square. He saw regiments of rebellious soldiers with "very familiar" people at the head. He saw cannon fire aimed at "rebels," which destroyed the hopes of the whole generation of Russian people who were confronted by the monster of tzarism.

The committee of inquiry on the Decembrists suspected Glinka of sheltering his former tutor W.K. Kückelbecker who had had time to escape. Fortunately Glinka easily managed to justify himself. Shaken by the events, he retired to Smolensk and Novospasskoye under the pretense of the wedding party of his sister, Pelagaya Ivanovna who was going to marry I.M. Sobolevsky.

But life was not that safe out of the capital either. Many families trembled with fear for the fates of their friends and relatives put into the cells of Petropavlovskaya fortress. W.K. Kückelbecker was arrested in Warsaw. A.S. Griboyedov was arrested too.

Alexander Griboyedov (1795-1829), a great Russian writer and poet, killed in Persia when on a diplomatic mission.

But time was passing. Transient passion for "pretty" Elisavetta Ushakova Mitskaya and amateur theatricals at the house of the general's wife Apukhtina distracted him a little. Glinka's wish at the time was to dream in the twilight at the grand piano and to read elegiac poetry by Zhukovsky, which moved him to tears. All this can be accounted for by the "romantic structure" of Glinka's nature. Wistful romances in the words of Zhukovsky *Svetit mesiatz na Kladbische* (*The moon is shining over the graveyard*) and *Bedny Pevetz* (*Poor Singer*) were an echo of the condition of his spirit at that time.

In May 1826 Glinka returned to Petersburg. A tremendous gallows was being constructed on the Kronverksky bastion of Petropavlovskaya fortress. Soon the best five sons of Russia of that time were hanged there on a foggy morning surrounded by the silence of hundreds of soldiers' bayonets. Soon their friends who held the same views were deprived of ranks and titles, put into irons and exiled to the Nerchinsk mines or incarcerated in the fortress.

Vasily Zhukovsky (1783-1852). Prominent Russian poet, Pushkin's older friend and advisor. Many of his verses inspired Glinka to write the music for romances.

Venevitinovs' house in a cozy Moscow side-street. There Pushkin first recited his tragedy "Boris Godunov," which made a great impression on Glinka.

In that same year Glinka issued only his piano variations on the theme of an Italian song *Benedetta sia la madre*, his first published composition. He was working at two more cycles of variations: on the theme of the opera *Faniska* by Cherubini and on a Russian song *Sredi Dolini Rovniya* which were already marked by his aspiration for filling virtuosity with melodies. He went to Moscow to see his schoolmates — N.A. Melgunov and S.A. Sobolevsky.

Having returned from his exile Pushkin read aloud his recently finished tragedy *Boris Godunov* at the houses of S.A. Sobolevsky, P.A. Viazemsky, the Venevitinovs' and, as V.V. Stasov supposed, "...maybe these enthusiastic days and hours spent in raptures by a crowd of Moscow intellectuals listening to *Boris Godunov* were the first and mysterious reasons that inspired *Zhizn' za tsarya* (*A life for the Tsar*). Note how close the epochs themselves are... Yes, Pushkin might be the father of *Zhizn za tsarya*, as he was the father of *Miortviye Dushi* and *Revisor*."

Glinka worked hard for some years after his return to Petersburg. He left public service to his father's displeasure who was very sorry his son had made "a skomorokh" ("a buffoon") of himself and devoted himself entirely to music. At that time Glinka did not try to write large compositions; he worked mainly at chamber — vocal forms: romances and Russian songs, arias and quartets with Italian texts.

M.L. Yakovlev, Pushkin's school-mate, was "a composer of well-known romances", as Glinka wrote about him in the *Zapiski* (*Memoirs*); Glinka gave the second voice to his romance — *Kogda Dusha Prosilas* ti" (*When you, the Soul were Begging*), and he introduced Glinka to A.A. Delvig.

The poet gave him the words of a song *Akh, ti notch, notch li, notchenka* (*Oh, you the Night, Dear Night*). Soon after that Glinka composed a Russian song *Dedushka, Devitsi raz mne Govorili...* (*Grandpa, Girls told me once...*), which Yakovlev "sang rather nicely." Playing music at his friends' house gave him a chance to listen to the music by classical and modern composers.

Concerts in the living rooms where new compositions were "tried" were replaced by serenades on the Tchiornaya river. As Glinka described it, amateur singers were singing fragments from operas by Boieldieu and other composers to the accompaniment of the composer playing the "small piano" on the deck of a launch decorated with lamps slowly passing beautiful country-houses. "Harmonious grand sounds" of the choir of trumpet-players were heard from the decks of the second ship.

Glinka acted as Donna Anna in an overture to *Don Giovanni* by Mozart at the house of Count V.P. Kochubey. Prince N.S. Golitsin remembered him as "a short rather funny figure in a woman's wig" who "sang contralto very well."

Glinka spent "almost all day long" with A.S. Griboedov. The writer gave him the melody of a popular Georgian song which later was the basis for one of Glinka's best romances *Ne poi krasavitsa pri mne* (*Don't sing thy songs of Georgia*) (on a poem by Pushkin). "He was a very good musician", — Glinka wrote about Griboedov in his *Zapiski* (*Memoirs*). *Lyrical Album for 1829* "was issued" thanks to Glinka and Pushkin's son-in-law N.I. Pavlischev. There were two romances by the young composer among mediocre pieces by his friends E.P. Shterich, M. Yu. Vielhorsky, N. Norov and others. One of them was *Pamyat Serdtsa* (*Heart's Memory*) — one of his most attractive compositions of those years.

Glinka spent the last "white nights" of that 1829 together with A.P. Kern, some of the Delvig family and writer Orest Somov at "Silvered by the Moon" Imatra waterfall in Finland. On his way back to Petersburg he listened attentively to a song of a coachman. He asked him to sing it several times, put it down and used it for a ballad in *Ruslan and Ludmila*.

Final scene of the opera "Ivan Susanin" staged in Sofia (Bulgaria), 1949.

Scene from the first act of the opera "Ruslan and Ludmila" on the stage of the Bolshoi Theatre in Moscow.

But soon after that Glinka fell ill and no pills of the "doctor born in Italy" could alleviate his suffering. His mother took him to the countryside but it did not help him at all. Glinka thought a trip abroad would give him a chance "to get rid of suffering and develop his musical talent." At first his father was resolutely against it but then understanding that his son's "health was quite out of order" and, with the doctor's advice, he gave his consent. The young composer's trip to Germany and Italy "was decided", all formalities "were settled" though not without difficulties; I.N. Glinka managed to settle everything gradually. He also vouched for N.K. Ivanov, a young tenor from a court choir, whom the composer took abroad to continue his musical education. They started off from Novospasskoye in bad weather — a long way to Smolensk, Brest and Warsaw. The travellers crossed the Russian border in the middle of May.

Chapter 3
UNDER THE SKIES OF ITALY

Tired after a long trip, the travellers had to stay in Dresden for several days. Glinka consulted Doctor Kreisig there. Having examined the composer the doctor advised him "to take the waters" at Ems and Aachen.

Snow and cold were soon replaced by May warmth. They passed Leipzig, Marburg, Frankfurt am Main, Mainz. If there happened to be a piano at a hotel where they stayed to have dinner or spend the night they started singing fragments of operas together with Ivanov and fellow-travellers ("Germans gathered to listen to us in small towns" — Glinka recollected later).

During their short trip on board the steamer along the Rhine, Glinka and Ivanov passed by the ruins of castles on the hills and small provincial towns whose roofs and Gothic steeples made a picturesque scene.

They walked all the way from Koblenz to Ems but three weeks of treatment only weakened the sick composer. However, hot baths in Aachen were useful and the beauty of Beethoven's *Fidelio* at the opera theatre drove Glinka to tears. However, he returned to Ems again to meet his Petersburg friend Eugene Shterich, a talented music lover, who served in the Russian embassy in Turin. Glinka stopped his treatment and together with Ivanov, Shterich and his mother made his way to Italy.

The travellers left Basel and proceeded through Solothurn and Geneva to Milan.

Their way led along mountain roads, through sparse growth of fir trees, overhanging cliffs and by summits sparkling with snow. Glinka wrote about the trip in his *Zapiski (Memoirs):* "We were together with Shterich in raptures with beautiful views of Switzerland." It was drizzling on the Simplon Pass. The slope began there.

A warm wind blew. The sombre fog cleared away. "In the evening the weather was delightful", flowering plains came to light and the travellers stopped on the bank of the light blue Lago Maggiore in North Lombardy. And the next day Glinka, Ivanov and the Shteriches came in their carriages to Milan. Milan was one of the music capitals in Italy at that time as that wonderful land "under the everlasting blue sky" was the motherland of Dante and Ariosti, Rossini and Donizetti. Glinka was not only attracted by the romanticism of contemporary Russian poets and painters but he was above all attracted by modern Italian music and a wish to develop as a composer.

The city of Marburg. Etching by V. Langue.

View of Ems, a health resort where the composer spent about three weeks in a vain attempt to recover from a serious illness.

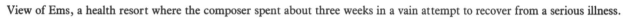

Scene from the second act of opera "Fidelio."
The beauty of Beethoven's music drove Glinka to
tears.

Milan

Maria Malibran, great Italian primadonna who sang the lead in the first performance of "La Sonnambula" by V. Bellini in Milan.

D. Batista Rubini, great Italian tenor, Malibran's partner on the first night of "La Sonnambula." His performance sent Glinka into raptures.

The composer was not mistaken in his expectations. The three years that he spent in Italy became years of thoughtful work and final development of his talent. Warm lyricism and the dramatic qualities of true human feelings in the music of theatrical performances by young Italian composers and most of all the plots taken from everyday life were new elements in operatic art for Glinka. There was a brilliant galaxy of opera singers — heirs of the best traditions of the 18th century who were appearing on the stage of Milan theatres. The performances with G. Pasta, G. Grizi, D. Rubini seemed something magical to Glinka.

The opening of the two main competing theatres in Milan took place on December 26, 1830. Glinka gave La Scala preference over Teatro Carcano. Sitting there in the box of the Russian envoy Glinka "was in raptures" with Rubini singing and the music by G. Donizetti at the premier of *Anna Bolena*. But he found the fascination of a melancholy refinement of music by V. Bellini closer to his heart. Glinka and Shterich with arms round each other "were shedding tears of raptures and tender emotions" at the first performance of *La Sonnambula* at the end of a carnival on March 6, 1831. He also heard the opera *Capuleti ei Montecchi* by the same composer in La Scala. Glinka based several piano and chamber compositions of his "Italian period" on the themes of the three operas: Variations (devoted to Shterich who died soon after that) and Serenade on the themes from the opera *Anna Bolena*; *Brilliant Divertissement* (for piano and string instruments) on the melody from *Sonnambula*, Variations for piano on the themes from opera *Capuleti ei Montecchi*, issued by the Milan music publisher G. Ricordi in 1831 and 1832.

Milan was magic itself. Glinka lived the first days of his stay there at a hotel near the famous cathedral. He admired the view of this magnificent cathedral made of white marble and of the city itself, "...the transparency of the sky, black-eyed women with their veils...". He brilliantly reflected the deep beauty of the Italian night in his barcarole-romance *Venetian Night* full of tremulous feeling of the joy of life.

Glinka then wrote two more romances on the poems by Zhukovsky and F. Romani and several cavatinas and arias in an Italian operatic style besides *Venetian Night* on the poem by I.I. Kozlov.

At the beginning Glinka thought he "didn't know vocal art well enough." According to the composer he gained knowledge in this field at Ivanov's lessons with A. Nozzari and J. Fodor — Mainvielle in Naples.

"The beautiful site" of the city, "transparent air, festive sunlight" fascinated Glinka. On his way to Milan he stopped at Rome to see Princess Zinaida Volkonskaya who had welcomed S.F. Schedrin, A.A. Ivanov, S.P. Shevirev, later Gogol and many Russian painters, sculptors, writers at her Palazzo Poli. Glinka met Hector Berlioz, a famous French composer, at her house.

Glinka usually stayed near Milan or at his favorite lakes in South Italy. He had a circle of acquaintances there and his new compositions were performed in the concerts at the houses of Doctor Brank and d'Filippi, a former military doctor. Such chamber compositions as "Big sextet" and "Trio pathétique" written by Glinka in Tremezzo and Milan in 1832 became remarkable evidence of his fully developed mastery.

He made a sad inscription on a music autograph: "I knew love only by the suffering caused by it." This desperate groan from the composer's troubled soul corresponds to a tragic finale motif-épigraph opening the first part. It appears again in the finale of the trio confirming the idea of the composition as a single whole and reflecting the state of Glinka's soul. He suffered morally and physically being far from his motherland.

In La Scala Glinka listened to *Semiramide* by Rossini and *Norma* by Bellini. In his constant wish to see new places and listen to new things, the composer travelled much through Italy. Besides the south of the country he visited Turin and saw the sights of "wonderful Genoa". In March 1833 Glinka was in Venice and visited the Doges' Palace. There he saw the paintings by Tintoretto. He also met Carl Brullov who was working at his painting *The Last Day of Pompeii* (it was their first meeting). With Bellini's personal permission Glinka visited the dress rehearsal of his opera *Beatrice di Tenda* which, according to Glinka, "was not a success."

The sea air and wind aggravated Glinka's illness and he hurried to Milan in the same stagecoach with the publisher Ricordi who had also been present at the rehearsal of the new opera by Bellini. Ricordi, the most prominent music publisher in Italy, had known Glinka for a long time. He had published Glinka's instrumental and vocal compositions. Several months before their first meeting November 1832 S.A. Sobolevsky wrote to S.P. Shevirev in Rome: "Now about Glinka. He sends his love to all of you. He imagines that he is recovering and he works hard at music. His published compositions are appreciated here. He also plans to compose a lot when he returns. Ricordi told me he considered Glinka equal to Bellini and Donizetti but more masterful in counterpoint combinations."

European music magazines also mentioned the name of the Russian composer with respect.

Although he found the fame flattering, Glinka was perfectly aware that only by having mastered "the subtleties of German music" would he be able to implement his creative aspirations. Besides, in the summer of 1833 Glinka's illness did not permit him to work much, though he wrote that he "thought over many things." Finally "torturing sensations" made him homesick and at the end of July he left Italy. After the brilliance of Italy he found Vienna dull. He listened to the music by I. Lanner and J. Straus, the father, but Dr. Malfatti's treatment did not help him. At the time Glinka's sister, Natalia Ivanovna Gedeonova, stayed in Berlin. He went to see her and "thus regained his good mood" on meeting her and her husband.

Soon Glinka occupied himself with intensive study under the guidance of a distinguished theoretician and teacher of music, Siegfried Dehn. It took him five months "to put in order" Glinka's technique of composition as well as his ideas about the art of composition and about musical art in general.

It must have been then that Glinka sent that remarkable letter to his friend whose name remains unknown. In the letter he most definitely wrote about his firm intention to create for Russian listeners a Russian opera on a Russian subject: "...In any case I want both the

Giulia Grisi and Giuditta Pasta acting as Norma and Adalgisa in the first performance of Bellini's opera "Norma" on the stage of La Scala in 1831.

Musical meeting in the Stuneevs' house. The last on the right is Maria Ivanova, M. Glinka's future wife. Drawing by P. Stepanov.

"Brilliant divertissement for pianoforte, two violins, viola, cello and double-bass on some of the themes from La Sonnambula by Bellini."

Giovanni Ricordi (1785-1853), founder of the world-famous music publishing house Ricordi & Co.

subject and the music to be national, so my countrymen would feel at home..." — the composer wrote.

It was with that idea that Glinka returned to Russia. The news of his father's death reached him in the capital of Prussia and terminated his stay there. In fact he was planning to return there soon. Now not only the lessons of Siegfried Dehn were attracting Glinka. It was also the image of a youthful singer, Mary. The composer mentioned in his *Zapiski (Memoirs)* that he "felt an affection which she seemed to share." They were soon writing to each other.

At the end of April Glinka returned to Novospasskoye in a carriage together with the Gedeonovs. But he did not stay long.

At the beginning of June 1834 Glinka left for Moscow though according to his words it was "rather pleasant to live in country silence with loving Mother and young sisters." He wanted to see N.A. Melgunov there and also to show the music lovers of the old capital that "he didn't travel in vain in Italy". Soon after the composer arrived in Moscow a kind of recital was organized at the house of N.A. Melgunov. Glinka sang and played his compositions and a talented amateur-singer, P.A. Barteneva and "string instruments" took part in the recital. When in Moscow he listened to the compositions by local composers and wrote a romance to the words of Moscow writer N.F. Pavlov *Ne Nazivay eo Nebesnoy* (*Do not call her Heavenly*). However the most important thing was that the desire to write a Russian opera was reawakened within him.

As the composer recollected he had neither "words" i.e. libretto, nor even any subject. For a while he decided upon Zhukovsky's *Mar'ina Roshcha* (*Marina Grove*) as a subject and even composed several pieces for it (they were partly included in *Ivan Susanin*.) Nevertheless the sugary sentimentality of its content devoid of real national character soon dissuaded him.

Glinka had to go to Petersburg to get a new foreign passport. And though "there was enough snow on the roads" he wasn't in a hurry to leave Petersburg and then "resolutely stayed" in Russia.

There were two important reasons for him to stay there. Glinka met Maria Petrovna Ivanova at the house of his relative A.S. Stuneev and her beauty more and more attracted him. He began to teach her singing. The girl took part in the Stuneevs' home concerts. According to Glinka they sometimes whispered for long "sitting on the sofa." Glinka's passion gradually grew and thoughts of Mary vanished. In a letter to his mother he confessed that the new feeling had "saved him." Now family happiness seemed possible for him.

In autumn 1834 Glinka's friend Yu. A. Koptev, "an enormously tall captain", brought to his place "a small man in a blue frock-coat and a red waistcoat. The man spoke in squeaking soprano. But when he sat down at the grand piano he turned out to be an accomplished pianist, and later a rather talented composer — Alexander Sergeyevitch Dargomyzhsky" — Glinka recollected in his *Zapiski (Memoirs)*.

The idea of creating a Russian opera which Glinka had cherished for a long time took a more concrete form. Later he recollected that although he had spent "most of his time at home" he had every now and then visited meetings at V.A. Zhukovsky's place: "every week a refined society gathered there. The society consisted of poets, men of literature and other people whose hearts were open to fine arts...

A.S. Pushkin, Prince Viazemsky, Gogol, Pletnev were frequent guests there... Prince Odoyevsky, Vielhorsky and others also attended those meetings. Sometimes instead of reading they sang and played the piano..." Zhukovsky not only sympathized with Glinka's aspirations but also suggested the heroic deeds of the peasant from Kostroma, Ivan Susanin, as a subject for his opera. The episode which took place in the "troubled times" of Russia at the turn of the 18th century often attracted Russian writers' attention. Composer C. Canos staged an opera on that subject in Petersburg Bolshoi Theatre in 1815. But it did not confuse Glinka. He briskly responded to the poet's suggestion. The scene in the forest had a definite impact on him; he found it very Russian and original.

Glinka wrote in his *Zapiski:* "I wrote the scene of Susanin with the Poles in the forest in winter. But before I started writing I had often read it aloud and imagined myself in the place of the hero so vividly that my hair stood on end and it made my flesh creep."

Glinka read *Doumi (Meditation)* and *Ivan Susanin* by Decembrist K.F. Rileev which was well-known in Russia in the first half of the 19th century. This would also influence his final choice of a subject for his opera.

Glinka started working with enthusiasm and without any delay. He rejected his own idea of composing an oratorio in three parts.

"...It seemed to be by magic. The scheme of the whole opera and an idea to contrast Russian music with Polish; eventually many themes and even details — all that occurred to me all at once", — Glinka wrote in his *Zapiski*. First Zhukovsky intended to write a libretto himself and even wrote poems for the epilogue but lack of free time made him "put" Glinka "into the hands" of Baron Rosen. He was a mediocre court poet "a German" who wasn't very good at Russian but this didn't embarrass the composer who resolutely made corrections of his clumsy verses and deleted flattering lines. Glinka named his composition *Ivan Susanin,* patriotic heroic tragedy-opera in five acts or parts.

N.S. Volkov, a pupil and friend of the composer, painted Glinka inspired and enlightened trustfully looking into the distance in the undoubtedly happiest period of his life at the end of 1834. Glinka himself said the portrait was "unusually successful" and a good likeness.

A year after his father's death he wrote to E.A. Glinka asking for her consent to his marriage with Ivanova M.P. The consent was immediately given. A modest wedding in the presence of a few witnesses took place in the church of Inzhenerny Castle on April 26, 1835. Soon Glinka with his wife and mother-in-law went to the Smolensk region to see his mother.

He was continuously thinking even as he rode in a carriage travelling in native Novospasskoye. "...I worked hard, i.e. put down everything ready and stored up" — Glinka remembered in his *Zapiski*. Every morning I sat down at the table in a large and bright sitting room of our house in Novospasskoye. It was our favorite room: sisters, mother, wife, in short, the whole family was already puttering about there and the more they spoke and laughed the quicker I worked. The weather was wonderful and I was working with the door open to the garden and breathing invigorating fresh air". He

Ludmila Shestakova (1816-1906), the composer's sister.

Pavlovsk railway station in the 1830s, where different social events, including musical concerts, often took place.

Maria Sherbatova, (née Shterich (1810-1879), Glinka's friend and pupil.

was happy the first year of his family life as everything "was going well".

Having returned to Petersburg he continued working at the opera with the same enthusiasm. It was already in early spring of 1836 that two rehearsals of the opera's first act took place at the houses of Prince B.N. Yusoupov and M.Y. Vielhorsky. Glinka gave the scores to the Director's Office of Imperial Theatres with a request, "If it's worth staging take it to the repertoire of the Petersburg Opera Theatre". A.M. Gideonov, Director of the Imperial Theatres agreed. However, Glinka had to sign an agreement waiving the right to any fees. Besides, the opera was renamed from *Ivan Susanin* into *Zhisn' za Tsarya* (*A life for the Tsar*). It had that name up to 1917 and when it was produced anew on the Soviet stage it was given its unique distinctive name.

Soon rehearsals started under the guidance of the Petersburg theatres music director, composer C. Cavos. Though he was the author of the opera of the same name he admitted that Glinka's music was better and dropped his opera from the repertoire. Glinka took an active part in the preparation too. It was decided to open the Bolshoi Theatre after its repairs with the new opera. The rehearsals were accompanied by hammers knocking. All of Petersburg, influenced by magazines and newspapers' articles, were eager to see the première.

It took place on 27 November, 1836. The house was full. The scenes of the opera followed each other: in the village of Domnino on the Volga River a choir of peasants sang about their native land and one could hear the wise words of old Susanin about a great menace threatening it; boastful speeches of Polish gentlemen could be heard at the ball given by a Polish king; in Susanin's poor dwelling his adopted child Vania sang his song and foreign invaders intruded into the festive preparations for the wedding of Antonida and Sobinin; these invaders took Susanin with them and he fearlessly went to face his death for the sake of saving Russia; the wailing of the wind and snowstorm were the background of his heroic death in the thicket to which he had brought the enemy. The triumphant choir *Slav'sa* ("Glory") filled the theatre with the sparkling happiness of peoples' victory in the epilogue on Red Square in Moscow. The mourning of Susanin's relatives was a sad cloud in the general rejoicing. Now, bells to the sound of the choir and the orchestra joined with new force in triumphant and forceful glorification of the native land.

O.A. Petrov sang the part of Ivan Susanin with remarkable expressiveness and dramatic effect. A. Ya. Vorobyova in the part of Vania was touching in her sincerity; a velvety timbre of her contralto gave a special beauty to the song *Kak mat' ubili* (*How they killed Mother*) and the trio *Akh,ne mne bednomu* (*Oh, not for poor me*).

"The music of the opera and the singing of Petrov and Vorobyova often touched me so much that I cried" — painter A.N. Mockritsky wrote in his diary.

"The audience welcomed my opera with enthusiasm, the actors played with zeal... Gedeonov organized the opera with great taste and luxury, it does him credit," Glinka wrote to his mother the day after the first night.

Yet, despite the loud applause and curtain-calls for the author the success of *Ivan Susanin* was not indisputable. The aristocratic part of the public contemptuously called the opera "coachman's music" for its Russian character (and this was undoubtedly the best praise). But the democratic part of the public filling the theatre at the following performances, believing in the existence of "Russian opera" welcomed it enthusiastically. Glinka's friend who shared his philosophy, V.F. Odoyevsky, came out with critical articles as a response to the malicious attacks of Bulgarin and his clique upon the opera.

The first night of *Ivan Susanin* in Moscow was on September 7, 1842, not long before the first night of his second opera *Ruslan and Ludmila* staged in Petersburg.

Ignatyev Monastery. Scenrey for
the opera "Ivan Susanin". Drawing
by M. Bocharov.

By the end of the year Glinka was offered the place of bandmaster in the Court Choir, and he accepted the offer. He was fond of his new activities, though he was aware of the fact that the director of the choir, A.F. Lvov, an envious and untalented composer disliked him. He paid no attention to this dislike, the more so because it was not manifested openly. So Glinka visited Lvov together with C.P. Brullov and N.V. Kukolnik and willingly listened to violin compositions by Haydn and Mozart in his performance.

Ivan Susanin was permanently in the repertoire and separate fragments issued by music publisher Snigerev were on the music stands in the houses where "they sang even if the slightest degree."

Program for the first night of M. Glinka's opera "Zhizn za Tsara" ("Life for the Tsar") on the stage of the Bolshoi Theatre, 1836.

Glinka often met V.A. Zhukovsky and A.S. Pushkin. But the composer wasn't "that happy" at home. His wife was a woman of fashion. She wasn't up to "high ideals" and was becoming more and more alien to him. Meanwhile new creative ideas were coming to the composer's mind and he needed peace and quiet. As a result of many family scenes Glinka more and more often stayed at his friends' brothers' house, N.A. and P.A. Stepanovs or Nestor and Platon Kukolniks, sometimes for several days. He could comfortably work there. And at the houses of the Vielhorskys and Odoyevskys he could meet interesting people, musicians and painters.

N.A. Stepanov, who knew Glinka very well, drew a series of drawings about him, some of them comic.

At the request of O.A. Petrov, Glinka composed and included into *Ivan Susanin* an additional scene of Vania on the text by N.V. Kukolnik for A. Ya. Petrova-Vorobyova in the autumn of 1837. The aria added features of robust virility to the image of the young man and became one of the most famous scenes of the opera. The singer was always a great success.

V.F. Odoyevsky wrote: "With Glinka's opera comes what they've been looking for in Europe for so long — a new element in the art and it starts a new period in its history: a period of Russian music. Let's say with hand on heart that such a heroic deed is not only a deed by a talented man but by a genius."

Scene from the fourth act of the opera "Ivan Susanin," previously named "Life for the Tsar."

Chapter 4
IN HIS HEYDAY

Once, probably in 1836, A.S. Dargomyzhsky met A.S. Pushkin at a literary party at the house of I.I. Koslov; N.V. Gogol and other writers were also present. They talked about the theatre and the poet said he wished to see the opera lyrical — a combination of "all miracles of choreographic musical and decorative art". Some time later Pushkin said at one of V.A. Zhukovsky's Saturday evening parties that he wished to change much in *Ruslan and Ludmila*. Glinka was anxious to know what in particular. But they didn't meet again. Having been seriously wounded by d'Anthés in a duel, Pushkin died on January 29, 1837.

Glinka was even more interested in the poet's intentions when the famous contemporary playwright A.A. Shakhovsky gave him "an idea" to write an opera, *Ruslan and Ludmila*. Glinka was carried away by the idea and hoped to plan it "under Pushkin's guidance". Thus the completion of Glinka's first great creation coincided with the origin of the second one.

Already, by the autumn of 1837, the composer played fragments from his new opera to his friends. Soon Glinka put down a well-thought plan of the opera in the copy-book presented to him by Kukolnik who "blessed him to write *Ruslan and Ludmila*." The plan became the basis for poems by many librettists — N.D. Markevich, M.A. Gedeonov, N.V. Kukolnik and above all by V.F. Shirkov, a talented writer and by Glinka himself. The Persian choir, cavatina of Goreslava, appeared one by one. Sketches of new scenes were being made. Already by March 1838 P.A. Barteneva sang the cavatina of Ludmila *Groustno mne roditel' dorogoy* ("I am sad, my dear father") with an orchestra at a large charity concert.

Glinka's work in the chapel certainly hindered him in his creative work. Though the results of his pedagogical activity gave him satisfaction, lessons in the morning reduced time for composition and as he was obliged to be present at public worships and at court festive

occasions, he had little time left for his own work. Lvov's thinly disguised hostility and constant fault-finding depressed Glinka. He needed breaks from his work on the opera. He was not happy in his family life either. His wife had "unreasonable whims" and "his mother-in-law hissed like a samovar" and "grumbled constantly". He got satisfaction only at his theatrical school. He composed the romance *Somnenie (Doubt)* for his "pretty pupil" Caroline Kalkovskay, full of languishing love and sincere sorrow.

Unfortunately "having quarreled with Gedeonov" as he put it in his *Zapiski* Glinka soon had to stop giving his singing lessons there.

Glinka went on a business trip to towns of the Ukraine and that relieved the monotony of his life. He was sent there to select boy singers for the court choir in spring 1838. Having got "money for travelling expenses" and "appropriate instructions" Glinka and his assistants started from Petersburg for Luga and then Pskov. They got to Chernigov through Smolensk, Novospasskoye and Novgorod-Seversky. They soon managed to find several children with beautiful voices and perfect pitch in a local seminary there.

In Pereyaslavl Glinka and his friends "ruthlessly robbed" the bishop's choir. They "took along with them" S.S. Gulak-Artemovsky from Kiev. "He was immensely loved by his friends; when he was leaving Kiev they cried saying goodbye to him", the composer recollected in *Zapiski*.

As the composer wrote in *Zapiski* he had made the estate of his old acquaintance, G.S. Tarnovsky Kachanovka, "the center of his operations". Taras Shevchenko had lived for some time there in his early years. The hospitable host accommodated his friends in the conservatory near the main building surrounded by ancient trees in the park, descending from the hill to the banks of the ponds and green lawns.

Semeon Gulak-Artemovsky (1813-1873), Ukrainian singer and composer.

It was from here that Glinka and his friends went to Pereyaslavl, Kiev, Romni, Poltava, Kharkov and returned to Kachanovka with children from the choir selected by them. They even succeeded in "taking out" from Kiev, baritone Semen Gulak-Artemovsky. Later he became a famous opera singer and author of the opera *Zaporozhets za Dunaem (A Cossack Beyond the Danube)*.

In Kachanovka during the intervals between his trips Glinka worked on Finn's ballad from the second act of *Ruslan and Ludmila*. Several times he sang it himself with the orchestra of Tarnovsky. The young painter V.I. Shternberg staying as a guest in Kachanovka painted Glinka composing music in one of the rooms of the mansion. It was then that Glinka for the first time listened to the march of Chernomor and the Persian choir *Lozhitsa v pole mrak nochnoy (The darkness of the night is falling on the fields)* from his new opera; Glinka had by chance taken with him their scores from Petersburg. Soon Shternberg also painted the "Blind-man's buff", where to the right one can see young choristers with their tutor G.I. Saranchin directing them.

The life in Kachanovka was enjoyable and not at all monotonous. The young nieces of the hostess, their governess and the daughter of the family doctor made their life more eventful and lively. They all went on trips, went to the neighboring estates and to dancing parties; they sang folk songs and among them Tchoomak and Ukrainian songs. Glinka composed the songs *Goude viter (Sing the wind) and Ne*

38

The game of "Blind-man's-Bluff." Picture by V. Shternberg. On the right is a boy's choir with their tutor G. Saranchin directing them.

Improvised concert in Kachanovka. Drawing by V. Shternberg. 1838.

Kachanovka. The hall where Glinka's compositions were played.

Quartet (A. Lvov, V. Maurer, G. Bilde, M. Vielhorsky). Lithograph by R. Rorbach.

Ukrainian song on the words of the poet Zabela "Don't You Twitter, Nightingale."

Ekaterina Kern, in marriage—Shokalskaya (1818-1879), to whom Glinka devoted his Valse-Fantasie for the piano. "She was not exactly beautiful, there was even some expression of suffering òn her pale face . . ." Glinka wrote in his "Memoirs."

schebeschi, soloveyko (Don't twitter, nightingale) to the poetry of V.N. Zabela. Glinka perceived the tuneful character of Ukrainian folk music so well that a few years later he had to defend his authorship in a letter to P.P. Dubrovsky.

Night concerts were organized in the conservatory where Glinka lived. Russian and Ukrainian songs were performed and friendly conversations lasted till the small hours. Shternberg was a success in making a pencil-drawing of these meetings and a portrait of the poet Zabela.

Having composed *A Hymn to the Host* in Tarnovsky's honor Glinka said goodbye to Kachanovka and his Ukrainian friends on August 13. He spent several days in Moscow and on September first in *Petersburg Vedomosty* his name was among those who had arrived in the capital.

In Petersburg Glinka not only directed the choir and composed the opera but he was also compiling *Collection of Music Pieces*. Glinka undertook it to popularize the works by Russian composers. Music parties on Thursdays took place in Glinka's flat in the building of the Chapel near the Pevchesky bridge across the Moika. Friends and acquaintances of the host and fashionable ladies who were friends of his wife gathered there. There were neither dances nor evenings when they played cards. But music sounded there instead, primarily solo-singing and ensembles. A. Ya. Petrova-Vorobeva, O.A. Petrov, P.M. Mikhailov and S.S. Gulak-Artemovsky, who was only commencing his career and lived in Glinka's house, sang at those parties. Sometimes Glinka himself sang his romances. His high voice wasn't beautiful in timbre, but, as A.N. Serov recollected, "a brilliant creator of music, Glinka was equally brilliant in vocal performance", which Serov found poetic and "too good for words". Princess M.A. Scherbatova, recently made a widow, also sometimes visited those parties. She was the niece of Evgeny Shterich, Glinka's friend, who had died young. She was very much admired by M. Yu. Lermontov.

On March 28 of the next year at his sister's home Glinka met Ekaterina Ermolayevna Kern, the daughter of Anna Petrovna Kern, whose name is sanctified by A.S. Pushkin's feeling for her. "She was not exactly beautiful, there was even some expression of suffering on her pale face...her clear and expressive eyes, her unusually slender figure (élance°) and a special kind of prettiness and dignity attracted me more and more", — Glinka wrote in *Zapiski (Memoirs)*. In summer his feeling was already "shared by nice E.K." (Ekaterina Kern).

The composer expressed his feelings for Ekaterina Ermolaevna in two compositions. The first of them is a charmingly elegant *Valse-Fantaisie* which is full of the elegaic poetry of love.

Orchestrated by the conductor G. German, according to contemporaries, it "fascinated" the listeners of the concerts in the Pavlovsk railway station and for many years it was known as *Pavlovsk Waltz*.

Romance *Ja pomnyu chudnoye mgnoven'ye (I recall a wonderful moment)* composed in 1840 is different in sentiment. It is inspired with the excitement of light exultation sometimes alternating with sad meditation. This romance is composed to the poem of A.S. Pushkin dedicated to Anna Petrovna Kern, mother of Ekaterina Kern. This composition by Glinka is a unique blending of the high poetry of the text and its equally high musical expression.

Glinka's family life went from bad to worse and he spent more and more time in the "fraternity" of Nestor and Platon Kukolnik. The circle of their friends and acquaintances soon became his own. There Glinka used to meet Carl Brullov who was at the height of his glory then. The composer's friends: brothers Peter and Nikolay Stepanovs, writer A.N. Strugovschikov, theatre doctor L.A. Gadenraih, I.A. Krilov, T.G. Shevchenko, V.G. Belinsky, I.I. Panaev, painters I.K. Ivazovsky, P.V. Basin, A.N. Mokritsky, Ya. F. Yanenko, sculptors N.A. Ramazonov and P.L. Stavasser, dramatic and operatic actors P.A. Karatigin, A.P. Lod, O.A. Petrov. There came guests from Moscow, too, T.I. Granovsky, a University professor, writer N.I. Nadezhdin, Kukolnik and Glinka's friend amateur-musician and "a famous playful fellow" K.A. Bulgakov.

They had "lively and various" talks, games of chess, sang in the choir. Nestor Kukolnik composed verses "just in case"; Brullov made comic sketches; Ivazovsky played oriental violin songs which Glinka used for *Ruslan and Ludmila*. The composer willingly played fragments from his opera himself. All that was a subject of a lively argument. Glinka greatly appreciated an artistic atmosphere and the friendship extended to him during that troublesome time at the house of the Kukolniks.

Glinka moved into the flat of P.A. Stepanov on November 6, 1839. Being sure in advance that envious Lvov would willingly "get rid" of him Glinka applied for retirement from the service at the chapel on December 7. As K.A. Bulgakov mentioned later "the most unhappy epoch" in the composer's life ended. All those sad events throughout 1839 distracted Glinka from his work on *Ruslan and Lud-*

Composer Mikhail Glinka and painter Carl Brullov. Cartoon by N. Stepanov.

"Writing the scores of an opera." Cartoon by N. Stepanov.

"Evening party at the Kukolniks." At the piano (left) is Mikhail Glinka.

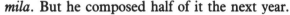

mila. But he composed half of it the next year.

The composer alternated his work on the opera with work on other compositions: *A Harmonic Gallery of Romances* — cycle *Proscha nie s Petersburg* (*Farewell to Petersburg*) on Nestor Kukolnik's verses was written in that creatively very fruitful 1840. According to *Khoudozhestvennaya gazeta* ("Arts newspaper") of September 1, 1840 such "full of life, reality and passion" and lyrical compositions as *Ritsarsky Romance* (*Romance of Chivalry*), *Barcarolle* and *Zhavoronok* (*Skylark*) were produced in that period. Glinka changed romance-bolero *Oh Deva chudnaya moya* (*Oh my wonderful maid*) into a piano piece and the orchestra of G. German performed it with great success with the instrumentation of the conductor himself in Pavlovsk in Summer 1840. *Poputnaya pesnia* (*Travelling Song*) which was in its way a farewell song was also included in the cycle. Nevertheless Glinka did not go abroad during those years. He started to compose music for the drama *Knyaz Kholmsky* (*Prince Kholmsky*) by N.V. Kukolnik in the middle of September, 1840. It took the composer less than a month to write the scores of such a remarkable composition. According to *Literatournaya Gazeta* ("Literature Newspaper") which abstained from comments on Glinka's music, the play staged in Alexandrovsky Theatre was not a success and that remarkably long creation collapsed at the very beginning with a thundering crash.

Having moved into Stepanov's flat the composer occupied a room which as he put it "was painted with caricatures and deviltry. When a coach would arrive, instantly the room would be illuminated, strange figures appeared for a moment one by one and a skull on the stove seemed to grin mockingly. At least it often seemed to me that it laughed at my sufferings. Then I slept badly and thought about my sad fate." And indeed new family troubles were in store for him.

Glinka sent in an application for a divorce to the Petersburg civil court. There began a conspiracy caused by Glinka's enemies in all possible ways.

It was forbidden for Glinka to leave the capital because of that. Hence he did not manage to see E.E. Kern in the Ukraine. With the passing years Glinka's passion for her faded. When "E.K." as Glinka called her in his *Zapiski (Memoirs)* returned to Petersburg they met "friendly but without former poetry and passion" or so the composer recollected.

In spite of all his troubles Glinka worked hard to finish the opera. He played fragments from it at the houses of the Engelhardts, A.N. Strugovschikov, the Vielhorskys, V.F. Odoyevsky, of poetess Countess Rastopchina. He also met Liszt, whose appearance in Petersburg in the Spring of 1842 "alarmed all dilettantes"; he met Dargomyzhsky and Brullov at the Karamsins. He showed his own drawings to "Great Carl." The painter inscribed under a landscape with a country mill: "Not a bad copy."

Sophia Englehardt (1805-1875), Glinka's acquaintance who together with her husband did a lot to promote Glinka's music.

Young composers and music lovers including Yu. K. Arnold and A.N. Serov came to Glinka's place for "instructions." Once Serov walked with Glinka along Admiralteysky Avenue. He was surprised to see Glinka exchanging greetings with so many acquaintances, which Glinka did politely but very seriously (by then he was well-known not only among musicians but also among many lovers of Russian music).

In a daguerreotype made in 1842 Glinka differed greatly from his previous picture. Standing erect with dignity he looks away as if he did not want to meet anyone's eyes. There are traces of thought and deep emotion on his face. He is clad in a well-tailored but not fashionable frock-coat. There is evidence of maturity that balanced hardships with his wise mastery of music.

Daguerreotype of Mikhail Glinka made in 1842 which is considered to be an exact resemblance of the composer in this period of his life.

Glinka gave the scores of *Ruslan and Ludmila* to A.M. Gedeonov, the director of theatres, and the latter agreed to stage it (he submitted the libretto "for approval" some time later). As P.P. Sokolov recollected, "the news about it reached the press...and the impatience of music lovers was growing rapidly." But Glinka had to overcome many hardships. The opera's way to the stage was thorny.

Orchestral rehearsals started in September. A. A. Roller painted sketches for the scenery which was Brullov's "idea". (Not all of the sketches were approved by the composer who wanted them to resemble Russian fairy tale settings and who decidedly rejected the scenery of Chernomor's castle in act four).

Glinka had to invite choreographer Titius to dinner to show him the Caucasian Lezghinka (dance). Writer P.P. Kamensky danced it so dashingly for him. "The wine had its effect on him" and though Titius, a Frenchman, didn't like Lezghinka very much he set to staging dances, Glinka recollected in his *Zapiski*. Glinka composed an overture to the opera which he was doing in a producer's room while rehearsals were going on.

Not long before the première T.V. Bulgarin, a reactionary critic and publisher of *Severnaya Pchela* (journal) "vexed" Glinka very much. He wrote a scornful article of a Russian opera company. It was the beginning of the series of "dirty tricks" that Bulgarin played

"The Flight." M. Glinka and musical critic A. Verstovsky cartooned as Ruslan and "evil" Chernomor from "Ruslan and Ludmila."

Franz Liszt (1811-1886), great Hungarian virtuoso and composer.

on the composer. Glinka exerted a great effort to calm irritated singers. A.N. Verstovsky, author of *Askol'dova mogila* (*Ascold's Grave*), who considered himself a founder of Russian opera showed his ill-will towards *Ruslan and Ludmila* too. (The composer's friend Bulgakov showed Glinka's "single combat" with Verstovsky in a comic drawing *Poliot* (*Flight*). Glinka was very sorry about many cuts in the music. However all the difficulties were successfully overcome.

"The splendor and magnificence of this play surpasses all we've seen at Russian theatres before" — Odoyevsky wrote not long before the first performance.

The première of the opera *Ruslan and Ludmila* was fixed on November 29 — the day of the sixth anniversary of the première of *Ivan Susanin*. O.A. Petrov (Ruslan) and M.M. Stepanova (Ludmila) starred again. But a young understudy acted as Ratmir instead of A. Ya. Petrova-Vorobiova who was ill. Tozi as Farlaf and Lileeva as Gorislava were not a success. According to contemporaries the scenery was "the epitome of luxury and elegance." Glinka had several curtain-calls. But hissing also could be heard. The second night "wasn't any better than the first" as Glinka put it. But on the third night Petrova had recovered — Vorobiova acted as Ratmir so fascinatingly and her voice sounded so wonderful that she was given a standing ovation. The opera had thirty-four nights during the season of 1842/43 alone.

After the first few performances when the aristocracy which only looked for entertainment formed the main part of the public, the "real Petersburg public" came. This "real Petersburg public" according to V.F. Odoyevsky came to the theatre to see and listen to "the magic opera" by Glinka, to appreciate the national character of its conception, in which fantasy and reality are so boldly interlaced; to perceive the beauty of the music filled with epic majesty in some scenes and sincere lyric poetry or seductive oriental beauty in others.

The efforts of Bulgarin, Zotov and their minions to reduce the success and the significance of *Ruslan and Ludmila* for Russian art met a decisive and efficient rebuff from O.I. Senkovsky and even more important, from V.F. Odoyevsky. "One can positively say that now no European musician has such fresh imagination capable for the whole fantastic opera — very original and new in everything" — Glinka's friend decisively wrote in *Otechestvennie Zapiski* (with the nom de plume of P. Bitchev).

F. Liszt gave his concerts in Petersburg in April and in May 1843 again. He attended one of the performances, watched it very attentively and then applauded demonstratively. He included his own masterly piano arrangement of Chernomor's March in the program of his concerts. He read the scores of *Ruslan* at the houses of Vielhorsky and Odoyevsky and willingly took part in a musical evening party at Glinka's place.

Liszt, a free-thinking Hungarian talking to a royal prince, Mikhail Pavlovitch who was a dull bureaucrat, called Glinka a genius in response to a declaration that the prince sent his officers to the Bolshoi Theatre for *Ruslan and Ludmila* instead of the guardhouse as a punishment.

The singers of Petersburg Italian opera which began to work in autumn 1843 also treated Glinka with deep respect. A "Triple Constellation of Stars" Pauline Viardot-Garcia, G. Rubini, A. Tamburini constantly and with great success sang the trio *Ne tomi Rodimiy* (*Don't tempt me, my Dear*) from *Ivan Susanin*. P. Viardot whom Glinka called a marvelous singer and considered himself her "ardent" admirer also successfully sang the cavatina of Gorislava and the aria of Ludmila with the orchestra of the Philharmonic Society. The Synod decided to lift Glinka's ban to leave Petersburg. His mother (E.A. Glinka) had decided to let him have a new trip abroad by that time. The preparations for a departure started.

Glinka was eager to leave Petersburg as he wanted to forget about the disgrace, the gossip, the envious spite of petty musicians and critics. Glinka hoped, as he wrote to his mother, "to forget about his grief" far away from everything and he believed that time would blot out of his soul the grief of recollections.

Being afraid of loneliness on his trip to Paris Glinka persuaded his relative Gedeonov to accompany him.

Glinka was pleased to get from Countess P.A. Bloudova an article by H. Mérimée about him on his birthday on May 21. The French writer wrote about the precious originality of the opera *Ivan Susanin* and that it was more than just an opera; it was "a national epopée."

That same day Ya. F. Yanenko, Glinka's close friend, made a plaster-cast of Glinka's face in his summer country house. Later he sculptured the composer's bust which contemporaries found to be a striking likeness.

Everything had been prepared for the departure by the beginning of June. Glinka together with E.E. Kern and M.S. Krzhisevitch came to see the Tarnovskys. His carriage came to the door. Glinka said good-bye to the ladies, called for F.D. Gedeonov and departed with the young French woman Adele Rossiniol.

The horses tore along the roads of the city. They passed stone palaces, then wooden houses, gardens. "The examination of passports at the columns of Moscow gates and then the golden spire of the Admiralty is far behind. ...We set out", — Glinka wrote in his *Zapiski* (*Memoirs*).

Mikhail Glinka. Bust by sculptor Y. Yanenko.

LEFT: Antonio Tamburini (1800-1876), Italian singer. RIGHT: Giovanni Batista Rubini (1795-1854), Italian singer.

Pauline Viardot-Garcia (1821-1910), prominent French singer in the part of Amina in V. Bellini's "La Sonnambula."

A symphony concert in the Paris Circus.

Chapter 5
YEARS OF WANDERINGS

Some time before approaching Luga, Glinka put down the song of the drayman which later became the main theme of Susanin. He wanted to say good-bye to his mother at Novospasskoye; then they stayed as guests at the home of Gedeonov's relatives in Bezzabotie; at the end of June they reached Warsaw; then through Poznán they moved in the direction of Berlin. There Glinka met Dehn, showed him the scores of his operas and the strict master of contrapuntal combinations was "extremely pleased" by the trio *Ne tomy, rodimy* (*Don't tempt me, my Dear*) from *Ivan Susanin*.

Travelling by post-chaise and by railway which had just been opened Glinka and his fellow-travellers passed through Cologne and Aachen, spent some time in Brussels; soon they passed Namur and Mons and passed the frontier of France. At last they reached Paris.

On a warm July day their heavy stagecoach passed by the frontier post of the city and found itself in the broad street of Montmartre. The beautiful and astonishing city surprised and captivated Glinka: "The largeness" of multi-story buildings, macadam carriage-ways, carriages going at top speed, horsemen riding down the street in the direction of the green circle of the Grand Boulevard, beautifully dressed passers-by, everything was lively and bright and so very different from the ceremonious strictness of Petersburg. "A tidy flat" overlooking "the best part of the Boulevard of the Italians" was easily found on the sixth floor of the house in Opera Lane. Glinka was overwhelmed by different impressions.

Russian acquaintances greeted Glinka warmly. Caricaturist M.L. Nevakhovich humored Glinka with "jokes and caricatures"; Petersburg acquaintance I.D. Norov, who had "a good store of money", constantly organized all kinds of entertainment. One of his friends always accompanied Glinka when he went sightseeing to see "the monuments and the suburbs of the city". He spent an autumn day in the Palace and the gardens of Versailles together with M. Yu. Vielhorsky and Elim Meschersky. The young poet had then begun the translation of the words of several romances by Glinka into French in the hope of publishing them in Paris; his untimely death that autumn prevented completion of the work. In the company of other friends Glinka saw the illumination of the Champs-Élysées and boat competitions on the Seine on the anniversary of the July days of 1830.

Soon after Glinka's arrival the journal "Revue et gazette musicale" informed its readers that M. Glinka "a famous Russian composer" was planning to spend the winter in Paris, and the staff of the journal expressed its hope that Glinka would compose "something for L'Opera-comique". But Glinka preferred the Italian theatre, "the best theatre in the world" according to him. In general, he did not find it possible to write for Paris theatres, in the first place, because of intrigues and in the second place because of his "Russian soul" which would not let him "compose things foreign to his nature."

Glinka soon got used to the French way of life, and assured his friends that it seemed to him that "he had always lived like that." Soon, however, the news that Liszt was giving concerts in Spain awakened in Glinka's soul his old wish to visit that country. Glinka began learning Spanish and made "good progress."

He was attracted to Spain mainly for artistic reasons. As he wrote to his mother on January 11/23, 1845 he wanted to get to know Spanish folk melodies, because "they are a little similar to Russian...and they will give an impulse to begin a big new work."

Glinka informed N.V. Kukolnik about his plans in more detail: "I decided to enrich my repertoire with several, and if I have enough strength, many concert pieces for the orchestra under the name *Fantasies pittoresques* (*Picturesque Fantasies*)...I believe that it is possible to combine the demands of art with the demands of the age and...to write pieces which are equally accessible to amateurs and ordinary people...In Spain I shall begin the formerly planned *Fantasies;* the originality of melodies popular there will be of great help to me...in any case I shall try to give my impressions with the help of the sounds."

Glinka did not spend a full year in Paris and among those he mixed with there and who gave their autographs in his so-called *Spanish Album* travelling with its owner throughout his journey were H. Mérimée, D. Ober, V. Hugo etc. But the most important and interesting figure Glinka encountered was Hector Berlioz. In fact they just renewed their old acquaintance; they had first met in Rome in 1831, when Berlioz lived in the villa of Medici as a pensioner of "Rome prize." He was in the heyday of his fame. The romantic flight of his artistic imagination, the bold search for and discovery of new forms and effects in orchestration were combined in him with the rapier wit of a satirist; all this attracted friends to him but also created enemies. However Berlioz' untiring energy and organizational ability did not allow any obstacle to prevent him from achieving his goal.

At first Berlioz was rather cold towards Glinka, but, soon, evidently having come to know the compositions of the Russian composer, Berlioz changed his attitude and became very friendly. Two years later Berlioz gave concerts in Russia and was cordially welcomed by Glinka's musical friends. Berlioz's help was of great importance to Glinka then. One of the aims of his stay abroad was to excite the Parisians' interest in his own compositions, to show them that Russian music and Russian composers existed. Therefore, when Berlioz offered to include some of Glinka's compositions into the programme of the third "musical festival" he was organizing, Glinka made a new orchestration of Lezghinka from *Ruslan and Ludmila* and asked the singer A.A. Soloviova-Verteil to sing in Russian the

Landscape with a water mill. Original drawing by Mikhail Glinka who was a good amateur painter.

Hector Berlioz (1830-1869), French composer and music critic.

aria of Antonida from *Ivan Susanin*. The concert took place on March 4/16 1845 in a huge and "exceptionally wonderful" hall on the Champs-Élysées. One hundred sixty musicians performed Lezghinka, and the singer, in spite of a certain roughness in "dangerous places" of the aria, was asked by Berlioz to sing the piece again in the fourth "festival." Glinka, as he said, had a successful debut; the commentary of the press was flattering and a day later, on March 6/18, he wrote to his mother about his intention to give a concert of his own "for the sake of the poor."

The preparations for the concert were troublesome. Besides fragments from his operas, Glinka decided to play *Valse-Fantaisie* with a new instrumentation. Being eager to satisfy everybody, he invited several famous performers to take part and... "the playbill turned out variegated."

Well-dressed Russian women turned an overcrowded Hertz Hall into a flower garden on the evening of May 29/April 10, 1845. However the expenses were not justified and Glinka had to borrow from V.P. Golitsin to pay his debts. The concert was a success though not without "variations"; tenor Marra, instead of the "frightened" Soloviova-Verteil, had to sing to Glinka's accompaniment an additional cavatina by Donizetti.

A complimentary article by H. Berlioz devoted to Glinka was published in "Journal des Débats" a few days later. In this article he put the name of the Russian musician "among the best composers of our time." There were other sympathetic and favorable comments in other Paris newspapers and magazines. Russia was informed of Glinka's success by the magazine *Illustration*, newspapers *Severnaya Ptchela* and *Moscow Vedomosti*. Soon after the concert Glinka wrote to his mother, "Maybe others will be luckier than me in their débuts but I am the first Russian composer whose compositions written in Russian and for Russians Paris music lovers came to know."

During his last month and a half in Paris, Glinka was busy preparing for his departure to Spain. By that time he believed he spoke Spanish better than Italian. He asked Evgeniya Andreevna to send him additional money for his trip. Glinka's Paris "majordom", Don Santiago, recommended to him as "an honest and efficient fellow", was in charge of all other matters.

Glinka, Don Santiago with his nine-year-old daughter Rosario started for Orléans in May 13/25, 1845 and then it took them three days to reach Pau by post-horses.

On seeing "ravishing southern nature" Glinka "cheered up". "Oaks, chestnut groves, poplar paths, fruit trees in blossom, huts surrounded by huge rose-bushes — all that was more like an English garden than ordinary country nature. Finally the Pyrenees with their peaks covered with snow struck me by their majesty", — Glinka described his travelling impressions in his letter to Mother from Pau "the last big city of France." Glinka and his fellow-travellers crossed the Spanish frontier on May 20.

Riding across "the highest mountains, by passes in inaccessible cliffs, over canyons where foamy streams ran and waterfalls dashed down, sometimes caught by thunderstorms, the travellers reached Pamplona, the first Spanish town. Everything was new for Glinka there: houses and their decoration, clothes of bright colors, "very queer dishes." Glinka mentioned in his first letter from Spain to his

Poster of the "Third Music Festival" under the guidance of Berlioz in which Glinka's compositions were performed.

mother: "On the journey I am not fastidious and eat what I am given but when I reach the place I'll arrange everything in my own way."

The Spaniards seemed to him kind and hospitable, sometimes hot-tempered but not for long. Glinka thought they were closer to his "nature" than any other "foreigners."

Glinka saw Spanish dances for the first time in the theatre. Soon a closer acquaintance with Spanish music began in Valladolid. In the evening "neighbors and acquaintances" gathered at the house of Santiago's people. Folk songs were sung and dances were accompanied by castanets there. Then Glinka heard the melody and variations of *Jota aragonese* smartly played to him by guitarist Kastilia. Soon in Madrid Glinka composed on its basis his famous *Brilliant Capriccio for big orchestra on Jota aragonese (Spanish overture 1)*.

Glinka successfully crossed this picturesque territory which had previously been infested with robbers and eventually reached Madrid. Soon he could appreciate that "small Petersburg", the beauty of its gardens, squares, fountains: the picturesque liveliness of street life, even the "barbarian show" of the bullfight. The Prado Museum — the richest collection of "magnificent pictures" by the Spanish painters which "has no equal anywhere" became the principal attraction for him. Glinka also saw the "sights" in the suburbs of the city: at Aranjuece, the most luxurious of the kings' residences and in picturesquely situated, semi-oriental Toledo with its narrow streets without windows "in Arabian style" and white marble cathedral with stained-glass windows. Glinka played the organ there in the silence of an autumn day. He also visited the palatial abbey at Escurial, the burial-place of Spanish rulers.

"Furious dance of Mikhail Glinka." Cartoon by N. Stepanov.

Madrid. Print from the drawing of an unknown painter.

The pleasant "quiet" life in Madrid, the healthy climate and being far away from Petersburg's petty troubles gave him an opportunity to forget unpleasant experiences and physical suffering. And though, as he admitted, he sometimes "had trouble" with his nerves it was the first time for a long period that he could do without a doctor's help.

Now he could calmly begin to study Spanish folk music. In the daytime and in the evening until late at night the sound of the guitar and singing could be heard in Glinka's room. He immediately put down in his "special note-book" "national" melodies and later used them many times.

Glinka decided to leave wet winter Madrid to find shelter in the south of Spain in ancient Granada which was full of Moorish echoes. Heavy clouds covered La Mancha and followed Glinka to the peak of the mountain ridge Sierra Morena. There was sunlit Andalusia with mountain slopes covered with green grass, lots of olive and orange groves, evergreen oaks and palms. "A tidy two-storied house with a belvedere" which Glinka and his fellow-traveller rented in the suburbs of Granada at the foot of the Alhambra was protected from the northern wind by the ancient tower Vermeja. Glinka saw through his windows roofs of the houses crowded together and the hazy distant mountains.

True to his intention to learn genuine folk music Glinka found rich material for his "work" in Granada. Soon after his arrival Glinka became acquainted with the "very talented" guitarist Murciano who "played masterly variations of the dance fandango" which Glinka jotted down on a sheet of music paper and soon sang with

"Mikhail Glinka studies Oriental music." Cartoon by N. Stepanov.

Mazurka composed in a mail coach at the end of May, 1852. Autograph.

"The escape of Mikhail Glinka from Spain to Warsaw." Cartoon by N. Stepanov.

Don Pedro Fernandes Nelasko Sandino. Pianist, guitarist, composer. Glinka's friend and companion on his many trips.

Ole Bull (1810-1880). Prominent Norwegian violinist and composer.

Dolores Garcia who was a famous folk singer. He also heard and saw singing and dancing at his new friends' homes when he "descended" to the town and was present at home entertainment or festive occasions, "watching people's customs." He called in gypsies to dance and learned to dance himself. "Legs obeyed but I couldn't do with castanets" — he wrote in his *Zapiski (Memoirs)*. According to the words of architect K.a. Beiné, Glinka spoke Spanish like a Spaniard by that time.

Getting ready to return to Madrid, in spring 1846, he proudly wrote to his mother that some of the pieces he was going to introduce to Madrid music lovers "will be of Spanish nature." Indeed as N. Kukolnik correctly mentioned in the magazine *Illustration* that same year "No one except Glinka can keep national melodies intact without disfiguring them by a strange sound..."

In Madrid, however, it was hardly likely that Glinka would be able to give a public concert. Now, more than any other time, his "rivals the Italians" that is, Italian opera, held "both the best theatre in Madrid and the Spanish audience".

The trio *Ah, ne mne bednomu (Ah, not Poor me)* from *Ivan Susanin* was the only composition by Glinka performed in Spain during the years of his stay there. It was performed at a court concert in autumn 1846.

But on his return he found the "necessary conditions" for his life in Madrid — absolute freedom, light and warmth. He also delighted in bright summer nights and the sight of public merry-making under the stars in the Prado. It resulted in the second Spanish Overture known as *Recuerdos de Castilla* or *Souvenir d'une nuit d'eté à Madrid*. This composition is a deep poetic reflection of Glinka's Spanish impressions in music, the same as *Jota aragonese*.

Glinka met a man who became his unfailing friend and companion for several years. One of his acquaintances introduced Don Pedro Fernandez Nelazco Sandino to him. Don Pedro, a man of a kind and agreeable nature, came from the provinces to perfect his knowledge of music. "Having been to the fair in Murcia together...ladies and girls in picturesque national dresses...gypsies danced three times for us...", Glinka and D. Pedro went to the south to Seville for the winter. According to Glinka's words Seville was "...the gayest" of all cities he had visited in Spain. And he wrote to his mother about Seville women dancers "all of this kind I've seen before can't be compared with local ones...", "National singers sang merrily in an Oriental way" at evening parties and at Miguel's and Felix's.

Glinka met the famous Norwegian violinist Ole Bull in Seville in spring 1847. Glinka and D. Pedro were "sorry" to leave the town in the middle of May.

After a short stay in Madrid they went through Saragossa and Pamplona to France. They rode along mountain paths among the Pyrenees cliffs and reached the Po River in June, 1847. They stayed three weeks in Paris and then in Frankfurt, Kissingen, Vienna, Warsaw — several days in each and at last — they arrived at Novospasskoye probably in early August. One more significant period in the life of the great composer was over.

The mild beauty of Russian nature in summer replaced the severe beauty of the plains and mountains of Spain withered by the heat. Orange groves on the banks of Quadalaviar River were replaced by the greenery of the lime park near the full Desna. Here was home after three years of wandering about Europe.

At first life in the country was "rather gay", L.I. Shestakova recalled later. Glinka's younger sister, Olga Ivanovna, was going to marry N.A. Izmailov. Relatives and guests were coming to the estate. "Everyday we made music for a long time". Glinka was healthy and sang romances willingly. He sang his own romances and those by Dargomyzhsky; sometimes together with Don Pedro he sang Spanish songs to the accompaniment of his guitar. He taught his sister Ludmila to handle castanets.

Soon, however, he began losing his appetite and slept badly; his nerves were "on edge" and things went from bad to worse. Before the wedding day Glinka went to Smolensk planning to go to Petersburg from there and to "trust himself" to the care of Doctor Heidenreich. A severe illness kept him in Smolensk all through the winter. L.I. Shestakova hurried to him from Novospasskoye. The illness subsided and brother and sister led "a quiet life at home". Each of them devoted several grateful lines to that period of life in their memoirs. "We didn't go out...but we received people...Brother was happy; the music, the singing with Pedro made the society more lively", — Ludmila Ivanovna wrote. "I didn't go out, in the morning I composed music", — Glinka recollected in his *Zapiski*. He composed several piano pieces then, and among them *Molitva* (*Prayer without words*) and Variations on the Scottish theme and two romances. The first of them *Milochka* (*Darling*) a clear recollection of Spain as the composer took the melody of Jota which he had heard in Valladolid for this romance.

The second romance *Ti skoro menia pozabudesh* (*Thou wilt quickly forget me*) is the words of the young poetess Yulia Zhadovsky and is a sad appeal to a lover, full of deep feeling and submissiveness to the unavoidable end; the romance became a new step in Glinka's development of the vocal-declamatory style.

The secluded and creative life of the composer in a snowy Smolensk came to an end in January 1848. It was interrupted by a ceremonial dinner in Glinka's honor organized in the auditorium of the Dvorianskoye Sobranie (the assembly of the aristocracy). It was followed by numerous balls and parties in the houses of local high officials. At those gatherings Glinka often "humored the public with singing and playing". No wonder that this "bustling life" drove Glinka to despair; he decided to go abroad. While he was waiting for his passport he went to Warsaw.

A small circle of friends and old acquaintances welcomed Glinka heartily in the Polish capital. "Our dear fellow-country man M.I. Glinka is staying with us as a guest", — P.P. Dubrovsky wrote to S.P. Shevirev on March 26, 1848. "We can't express our admiration of his musical compositions, which he himself performs. You have heard him, so you must know. Now he is planning to compose 'Ilya Murometz'..." Together with Dubrovsky Glinka read the writings by Russian authors and Shakespeare; he spent "nice evenings" with the Koniars and with amateur singers. Glinka bought some birds and kept them in his flat in Rimarskaya, "There were nightingales, redstarts and so on...". In the evening guests also sometimes gathered at Glinka's, "there were also two tame hares which sometimes drummed against the guests' feet", — Glinka recollected in *Zapiski*.

Olga Izmailova-Glinka (1825-1859). Composer's younger sister.

Pavel Dubrovsky (1812-1882). Slavonic philologist and writer.

But Glinka's "pleasant life" in Warsaw began with an unpleasant collision with the Polish vice-regent I.F. Paskevich-Erivansky. The prince, who was a petty tyrant, "rode into" Glinka and Don Pedro who didn't know Russian customs and didn't take off his hat when the prince was riding by. However, soon he learned that he himself had insulted Glinka and he tried to make amends by inviting Glinka to his palace. It was not the hearty welcome or Cahetian wine that attracted Glinka to the prince's palace but the orchestra, although it "wasn't particularly good".

But with this orchestra close at hand Glinka got a chance to study, to listen to classical music and music of his own from *Ivan Susanin, Jota Aragonesa, Molitva, Prayer without words*. For this orchestra he composed a symphonic piece based on four Spanish melodies. This piece *Vospominanie o Kastillii* (*Recuerdos de Castilla*) was the first variant of his Spanish Overture 2.

During that time of creative peak in the summer and autumn 1848 Glinka, "getting down to business", composed such wonderful romances as: *Slishu golos tvoy* (*When I hear thy voice*) is the words by M. Lermontov, *Zazdravny Kubok* (*The Goblet*), to the poem by A.S. Pushkin, jokingly dedicated by him to "La Veuve Clico" in other words to champagne; and the best of them *Pesn' Margariti* (*Gretchen's Song*) is the words by Goethe. By its depth and tragic expressiveness this song-romance belongs to the vocal lyrics of the last period of Glinka's creative work.

Exercises in counterpoint composed by Mikhail Glinka.

It was with the orchestra of Pashkevich, which sometimes gathered to rehearse in Glinka's house that the composer, according to P.P. Dubrovsky, "tried several parts" of his great new composition *Wedding Song and Dance Song*, afterwards renamed *Kamarinskaya*. One can't overestimate the importance of this composition for the Russian symphonic school. P.I. Tchaikovsky said about it: "The whole of it is in *Kamarinskaya* like the whole of the oak-tree is in acorns."

The composer gave in *Kamarinskaya* a bright and poetic picture of the life of Russian peasants. It was possible owing to the composer's deep penetration into the character of the Russian people which found its expression in its national music, the composer's rich creative imagination and his brilliant musical genius.

The tune of the wedding song *Iz-za gor, gor visokih (From behind the Mountains, High Mountains)* warmed by the sincerity of the lyrics is masterfully combined with the intonations of the gay dance tune *Kamarinskaya*, full of playful mischief. In the course of their development, full of the spirit of folk music art, new variation-pictures spring up and form the logical whole of the immortal *Russian scherzo* by Glinka.

The first edition of the score of "Kamarinskaya." Title page.

FACING PAGE, TOP: "Russkaya Plaska" (Russian Dance). Cheap popular print of the middle of the 19th century. BOTTOM: "Kamarinskaya." Fantasy for a symphony orchestra. Autograph.

Adam Mickiewicz (1798–1855)
Great Polish poet.

In November 1848 Glinka decided to return to Petersburg to meet his mother who was staying there as a guest of her daughter Elizaveta Ivanovna Flory. Taking his leave of his pupil A.K. Vogak he gave her as a present his portrait drawn in pencil by the painter Ivan Palm. The young singer said that the composer closely resembled his image in the drawing. He wrote on the drawing in French: "November 7/19, 1848 on the day of my departure from Warsaw to the lady who wants to remember me." This image of Glinka who has grown older and has put on weight differs greatly from all his preceding portraits; one can see the expression of fatigue on his pale, puffy face.

In fact, soon after his arrival in Petersburg Glinka fell ill. Fortunately two visits of Doctor Heidenreich were enough for him to overcome the illness. Glinka lived then in the building of the College for the deaf and dumb with his mother and two married sisters and though their place was "not roomy" their life was "pleasant".

When he had recovered Glinka attended the 50th anniversary of V.A. Zhukovsky's literary activities, paid visits to V.F. Odoyevsky whose advice he followed by renaming his Wedding Song and Dance Song Kamarinskaya. He also visited the Bunins and the Girses, where "with great enthusiasm and expression" he sang his romances and met pianist A. Henselt who was very popular at that time. In

Mikhail Glinka. Drawing by I. Palm.

the spring he saw V.V. Stasov, and soon N.A. Novoselsky introduced him to "the young people and writers of the new generation" — the circle of M.V. Petrashevsky (in the same year ruthlessly annihilated by Nicholas I). Glinka's playing and singing could be heard by F.M. Dostoevsky then. In February of the same year, evidently at V.M. Kazhinsky's, Glinka met a famous Polish composer S. Moniuszko.

Early in May Glinka returned to Warsaw again. And his journey there along a spring road in sunny weather was most enjoyable. This time his stay in Poland lasted over two years. However, this period was not so fruitful for his music as the first one. A lively but dissipated life in the company of his friends at the beginning of his stay in Warsaw distracted him from his creative work. At that time his musical impressions were confined to the playing of A. Freier, who masterfully performed J.S. Bach's compositions.

Later there were meetings with his friends such as M.I. Kubarevsky, through whom Glinka came to know Emilia (Mitza) Om, who inspired "a poetical feeling in him". Then there were P.P. Dubrovsky, A. Ya. Rimsky-Korsakov, S.A. Sobolevsky, his talks with Polish composer K. Kurpinski, and his music lessons with gifted girls Izabella and Julia Grünberg put an end to his apathy and reawakened him to "music activities".

In autumn 1849 Glinka dedicated to Emilia Om his romance *Rozmova (Beseda) (A Talk)* to the words of the Polish poet A. Mickiewicz; then followed the composition of romances *Adèl* and *Mary's Song* to the words of A.S. Pushkin and other compositions. The new version of the second Spanish overture *Vospominanie o Kastilii (Recuerdos de Castilla)* then received the new name *Summer Night in Madrid* which the composer completed during the last months of his stay in Warsaw. They were darkened for Glinka by his mother's death. Evgenia Andreevna died in Novospasskoye on May 31, 1851.

A countryside view in the suburbs of Warsaw. Drawing by I. Palm. (from M. Glinka's album).

In the second part of September Glinka left Warsaw with Don Pedro.

Glinka arrived in the Russian capital on September 24, 1851. He found that the capital had changed greatly. After the Petrashevsky cause which frightened Tzar Nicholas reaction intensified and in Petersburg, as well as throughout Russia, free and fresh ideas hardly glimmered. But the city was being decorated. St. Isaac's Cathedral was being completed, the horses by Klodt on Anichkov bridge reared, the Hermitage was going to open the doors of its museum. However, the doors of its richest collection of painting and sculpture were for a long time open only to a "selected" society.

However, Nestor Kukolnik was no longer in Petersburg; Carl Brullov, who was very ill, was dying in Italy. The circle of old friends disintegrated and a new one appeared. Here lies the significance of the composer's stay in the capital.

Now Glinka was surrounded there by the new generation of Russian people, the thinking youth of 1840-1850's: brothers V.V. and D.V. Stasovs, A.N. Serov, V.P. Engelhardt, later M.A. Balakirev, pianist and composer M.A. Santis, musicians and ardent lovers of music, especially classical music. According to the words of V.V. Stasov "all through his life Glinka better and better understood the music of the greatest and the strictest composers: Beethoven, Bach, Handel, Gluck, old Italians were becoming his favorites... The scores of Gluck's operas didn't leave his piano." Extracts from them, as well as the operas by Cherubini, overtures by Beethoven and Mendelssohn constantly sounded in his house. He asked his friends to perform them in duet, and sometimes he asked four and even six performers to play them. One day they played for him his own *Jota Aragonesa* arranged for two pianos by Serov and Engelhardt under the guidance of Glinka himself.

Glinka granted Shestakova's wish to write down the polka which according to his words he had "played in duet since 1840." Soon he gave it to publisher K.F. Golts under the name of *Pervonatchal'naya Polka* (Original Polka) and it was issued that spring "for the sake of the poor, supported by the Charity society."

L.I. Shestakova organized a charity concert which mainly consisted of Glinka's music on April 2, 1852 "for the sake of widows and orphans" of the Philharmonic Society. Glinka underlined in his *Zapiski* "It was done by my sister — not me".

That evening the composer heard for the first time his compositions *Souvenir d'une nuit d'été à Madrid* and *Kamarinskaya* performed by an orchestra conducted by C. Schuberth. Glinka received a great ovation from the orchestra at the rehearsal and many musicians embraced him heartily.

Meanwhile Glinka obtained a foreign passport. Petersburg's best photographer Levitsky took photos of both Glinka and Shestakova together and separately a few days before the departure. Probably it also happened at the request of Ludmila Ivanovna. The composer looks stout, older than his age, with long grey hair and he is dressed in a comfortable suit. Glinka seems to be listening to some inner music.

In honor of his name-day he let free singing birds, two chiffchaffs, which had amused him in winter time. Two days later his

Alexander Serov (1820-1879). Composer, music critic.

Vasily Engelhardt (1828-1915). Astronomer; music-lover promoting compositions of Russian authors— his contemporaries, a great admirer of Mikhail Glinka.

Mikhail Glinka with his sister Ludmila Shestakova.

friends and acquaintances, among them Ludmila Ivanovna, took leave of Glinka and Don Pedro. The two were going to France but the composer's final destination was Spain.

It was spring again. The forests were green and full of birds singing. But there was less striving for new places and more joyful anticipation of new impressions in the heart of the composer.

Fortunately a "rather beautiful lady" joined them in the coach. She added charm to their long journey to Warsaw. It was in the stagecoach that Glinka composed for her *Malen'kaya Mazurka* (*Mazurka*) "composé en diligence", a poetic piece in Chopin's style.

Giacomo Meyerbeer, always well-mannered and polite, came to see Glinka at the hotel on the day of his arrival in Berlin. In their talk he incidentally asked, "I wonder, Mr. Glinka, why we know you as a famous composer but we don't know your compositions."

"It's only natural," Glinka answered, "I am not in the habit of advertising my own work."

They proceeded through Hanover, Cologne, Strasbourg and Nancy where they saw museums, cathedrals and other sights by railway and in "tormenting stagecoaches" to Paris which they reached on July 1, 1852. "Much, much of the old echoed in the heart". "A nice city, a magnificent city, a good city — small town Paris" — the composer exclaimed in his letter to Shestakova written the day after his arrival. True, Glinka had a different opinion of the French capital by the end of his stay there. He spent his first evening in Paris on the Champs-Élysées in the society of H. Mérimée who soon became his permanent companion in seeing museums and walks in the old part of Paris. All that stay in Paris was marked by meditation on

Giacomo Meyerbeer (1791-1864). German composer and conductor.

Paris. Hotel de Clunie. Print by Trichon from drawing by Tieron.

64

the fate and ways of the development of Russian art and studying antiquities.

He saw the Louvre together with Mérimée — "a miracle — as a collection of pictures and marble sculpture". "Incomprehensively beautiful pictures by Veronese", "perfect works" by Raphael, Titian, Correggio, Poussin and antique statues of Venus. The Tiber, in particular, made an unforgettable impression on Glinka. They saw a collection of medieval trellis, stained-glass panels, lemon enamels in the Gothic Hotel de Clunie not far from the ancient cathedrals.

They wandered along the crooked lanes of the Cité near Notre Dame de Paris, the narrow streets of the Latin Quarter and the Marais.

Glinka's attempt to leave for Andalusia failed. He wrote in his *Zapiski Memoirs* that his "ailment" prevented him from visiting Spain. "Continuous suffering" from "irritated nerves" was experienced in a car on the way to Avignon and then to Montpelier. Such discomfort allowed him to go only as far as Toulouse. Three weeks later he and Don Pedro returned to Paris. "I grew absurdly old, dear sir", Glinka said to Dubrovsky about that episode from his life abroad.

They were leading an uneventful "stay at home" way of life. Glinka made music in the sitting-room of H. Merimée's friends Mr. and Mrs. Dupors; he gave lessons to young girls in singing, Italian "in particular." He also met Russian friends and acquaintances — writer and music critic N.A. Melgunov, actor V.V. Samoylov and traveller A.D. Saltikov.

Glinka was glad to learn that his sister Ludmila Ivanovna Shestakova had given birth to a daughter, Olenka, in March 1853.

However, that period was fruitless for the composer's work. He began work on the symphony *Taras Bulba* which he had intended to do long before in September 1852 but soon he gave up the idea. As Glinka wrote in his *Zapiski (Memoirs)* he couldn't "get out of the German way" in composition "while working at the symphony that is not to follow the canons of German classic symphonism." But he failed to find his own "way" in this particular case.

A year later Glinka was homesick in spite of the quietness of Parisian life, long days filled with reading classic literature, walks in the gardens of the Tuileries or in the Botanical gardens, the climate "dry and moderate." Informing Ludmila Ivanovna in 1852 that he couldn't continue working at his compositions, he wrote, "I am sure that I am capable of something only in my Motherland". "I am bored in a foreign country" — Glinka complained to her in summer 1853. His nostalgia had grown by the end of the next year. Eager to return to the Motherland he bombarded his sister with commissions to find a winter flat in Petersburg and rent a summer cottage in Tsarskoye-Selo. The Crimean war which broke out in the spring of 1854 sped up the departure of Glinka and Don Pedro "from Babylon, i.e., from Paris."

Glinka, in spite of his poor health, wished to see any opera by his favorite Gluck on the stage in Berlin. His wish came true thanks to the director of Royal Theatres and an agreement of singer Louisa Küster who starred in the opera. "Heard Armide — enough" — Glinka wrote in rapture to Odoyevsky after the performance. In that letter he imitated his boarding-school teacher Kolmakov.

Henri Mérimée (1807-1897). French man of letters. Drawing by L. Kouderk from M. Glinka's Spanish Album.

The hall in Tomilova's house in Ertelev side-street in Petersburg. Drawing by I. Vrangel.

Breslau, Chenstokhov, a few days' delay in Warsaw as his leg ached and, at last, Petersburg appeared in the window of a mail-coach. "...I took a nap and Pedro having learned my sister's address in Tsarskoye-Selo took me there half asleep. I found my sister Ludmila Ivanovna and my little god-daughter in good health", Glinka finished his *Zapiski*. And added: "The end".

Indeed Glinka's *Zapiski (Memoirs)* ended at that point. Unfortunately a very creative period of the great composer in Petersburg 1854-1856 wasn't included. It was then on his arrival from "strange lands" that Glinka at the request of Ludmila Ivanovna "started writing his own biography". He stopped writing it at the point of his arrival at Tsarskoye-Selo in May, 1854. Perhaps he didn't expect impressions equal to those he had described with such spontaneous liveliness earlier in his life. As they are a frank and true description of the composer's life and of the epoch itself, Glinka's *Zapiski (Memoirs)* belong to the most significant literary monuments of the world's literature of Memoirs.

Glinka "lived well" at Meyer's comfortable country-house with a large garden near the parks and under Shestakova's care. He wrote *Zapiski* or instrumented *Invitation to the Dance* by Weber. He played with little Olenka on the carpet of the balcony for a rest.

Friends from Petersburg usually came in the daytime. They had a walk in the parks or in the conservatory. There were music evening parties too. Once V.A. Kologriviv, I.N. Pikkel and other musicians played Glinka's youth quartet quite unexpectedly for him and he didn't recognize it.

"The torture of martyr Beethoven." Cartoon by N. Stepanov.

Daria Leonova (1829-1896).
Russian singer, Glinka's pupil.

Only once, and it was at Ludmila Ivanovna's request, they went to Pavlovsk to listen to the local orchestra.

At the end of August, "when it grew darker in the evening", Glinka began to urge Ludmila Ivanovna to return to the city. They rented a large flat in the house of Tomilova in Ertelev by-street, now Chekhov street. As Ludmila Ivanovna recollected, "there was a lot of music there. Everybody seemed to come to play and sing there. And brother was often animated and sang. He didn't compose much." In fact Glinka composed little in those years and was mainly occupied with the arrangement for signing with the orchestra and orchestration of other pieces. Thus in his *Molitva (Prayer without words)* arranged for the piano, Glinka "used" the words of the poem by M. Lermontov. He arranged *V minuty zhizni trudnuiu (In life's hard moments)* into a vocal-symphony piece for contralto solo voice, chorus and orchestra and gave it to his pupil, D.M. Leonova, a singer of the Russian opera. It was for her concert the next year that Glinka for the third time and "with deliberate improvement and intent" arranged *Valse-Fantaisie* devoting it to"... his old friend K.A. Bulgakov". The composer's last symphonic work was *Torzhestvenny pol'sky (Festival Polonaise)* on a Spanish bolero melody.

Inspired to compose an opera on the subject of the drama from the Russian common peoples' life *Dvumuzhnitza (A Woman having two Husbands)* by A.A. Shahovsky, Glinka sang and played to his friends musical extracts from it. Unfortunately in 1855 Glinka cooled towards the work. In spite of V.V. Stasov's "attempts to talk him into completing it" the composer "put it off."

Glinka's circle of acquaintances remained approximately the same as they were in 1851-1852. As in old times the hospitable house he shared with Ludmila Ivanovna became one of Petersburg's music centers. On Fridays they had "wonderful music parties." According to P.P. Dubrovsky every day "actors got together there." K.B. Schubert, L.W. Maurer with his sons "humored" Glinka and his friends with classical music. P.A. Barteneva, A. Ya. Bilibina, I.L. Grünberg, M.V. Shilovskaya, V. Ferzing sang there. Quartet meetings were held; they played extracts from Glinka's operas with eight hands; V.P. Engelhardt, D.V. Stasov, P.P. Dubrovsky and others were frequent quests.

In bright spring weather Glinka, together with D.M. Leonova, drove in a carriage about the city and the islands. They drove as far as the seaside and the end of Krestovy island from where there was an expansive and "magnificent view". Glinka did not like the monument to I.A. Krilov in Letny Sad (Summer Garden), but he found the hot-houses in the Botanical gardens on Aptekarsky island "very nice." At home Glinka played a lot with his niece and told her fairy-tales; he also sang with her. Don Pedro left for Paris "to get married."

Early in 1856 Glinka composed his last romance *Ne govori chto serdzu bol'no (Do not say the heart is sick)* based on the poem of his old Moscow acquaintance N.F. Pavlov; the latter begged him "on his knees" to compose music to his words. "The whole world is scolded in it, the public too, and I like it", — Glinka remarked in one of his letters to Nestor Kukolnik.

His irritation is understandable. The democratic art of the composer won new admirers while the reaction of official circles to his

Mikhail Glinka. Drawing by V. Samoilov.

1853

music remained hostile. As a result one of his two operas was performed on the stage and even this one, *Ivan Susanin*, was performed only on festive occasions. When publishing Glinka's romances, businessman and editor Stellovsky allowed himself many liberties with the text. This also caused Glinka many unpleasant moments. But the most distressing thing for the composer was the enmity of critics superficially and smugly discussing his compositions. Their ideas were opposed to the general tendency of the young Russian national school.

Glinka's health grew worse. "I am desperately ill", he wrote to Bulgakov in March 1856. "...I live on hope to run away to the West at the end of April," Glinka wrote to him several days later. He found lessons in counterpoint with Siegfried Dehn in Berlin a necessary thing in order to combine as "in a happy marriage" the western fugue and "the conditions of our music." Early in April in the newspaper "Sankt-peterburgskie Vedomosti" ("St. Petersburg News") three articles were published about Glinka's departure abroad.

On April 25, 1856 photographer S.L. Levitzky took the last photo of him. It is a "remarkable" though hardly representative portrait. In an attitude full of dignity, with his hand behind the lapel of his suit, his eyes looking into the distance, Glinka appears in the photo as "the great composer of the Russian land."

No wonder it was from this photo that a popular contemporary print was taken.

FACING PAGE:
Mikhail Glinka. Photo by S. Levitsky. The last photo of the composer.

On April 26 Glinka gave to the young pianist and composer M.A. Balakirev, who had come to Petersburg from Nizhni Novgorod a year before, the theme of a popular Spanish march as material for composing a symphonic overture. According to L.I. Shestakova, the great composer foresaw "a brilliant future for him" and even hoped "that in the course of time he will be a second Glinka."

On April 27 at half past twelve p.m. contrabass player A.B. Memel in whose charge L.I. Shestakova had left Glinka on their way to Berlin, called for Glinka in a carriage. V.V. Stasov also took his seat in the carriage. After a short farewell the coach disappeared in a cloud of dust.

Early in May the tired travellers arrived in Berlin and Memel gave Dehn charge of Glinka; Glinka was "in the best condition", and Dehn sent to Ludmila Ivanovna a humorous receipt. The last short period in the great composer's life had begun.

Glinka described his life in Berlin as "good...because he had business to attend to", "free...because they had nice things to eat", "quiet...because he led a stay-at-home life and didn't seek new acquaintances." In this way in his letter to K.A. Bulgakov on June 27, 1856 Glinka described his life in the "kind and nice" family of the Millers, with whom Dehn had found him accommodation. Monotonous days were filled with the study of counterpoint, studies of the scores of classical composers, going to opera performances and concerts, walks about the city and its countryside.

Meetings with friends and old acquaintances passing through Berlin made life more lively. Among them there were V.F. Odoyevsky, Matv. Ya. Vielhorsky, A.G. Rubinstein and also the former "Pavlovsk conductor" J. Gungl.

Berlin. Print and drawing by H. Barkamp and E. Rein.

M.I. Glinka composing his opera "Ruslan and Ludmila." Picture by the great Russian painter Ilya Repin.

Glinka did not want to write "dissertations about music." But in his letter written on July 10/22, 1856 to composer V.N. Kashperov, whom he called jokingly "my dearest son" and who followed his advice for some time, Glinka wrote about his esthetic views on the correlation of content and form in art.

"All arts, and, therefore, music, demand:

1) Feeling, "L'art, c'est le sentiment." Art is feeling — this comes from inspiration.

2) Form. "Form means beauty," i.e. proportionality of parts for the composition of a single harmonious whole.

Feeling gives the main idea; form dresses the idea in a decent and fitting *riza*.

Feeling and form: they are the soul and the body. The first is a gift from Heaven, the second is acquired by hard work, and an experienced and intelligent guide is of great help."

On November 8, 1856 in the Opera theatre Glinka met Meyerbeer who told the Russian composer about his admiration for his music. Not long before Meyerbeer had listened to *Kamarinskaya* in Spain. At his request Glinka sent him five extracts from *Ivan Susanin*. Meyerbeer chose from them the trio *Akh, ne mne, bednomu* (*Oh, not for poor me*) for the court concert. Glinka himself organized the rehearsals "with the piano."

Johanna Wagner (1828-1894). German singer.

CONCERT

im

Weissen Saale des Königlichen Schlosses

zu Berlin

am 21sten Januar 1857.

1. Ouverture zur Tragödie „Coriolan" . . . . Beethoven.
2. Scene aus der Oper: „Il trovatore", gesungen von Frau *Herrenburger-Tuczeck*, Herrn *Mantius* und dem *Chor* . . . . Verdi.
3. Variationen für die Violine, vorgetragen und componirt von . . . . Bott.
4. Finale aus: „der Sturm" nach Shakespeare,
   a. Abend-Gebet der Schiffs-Mannschaft . . . .
   b. Der Sturm auf dem Meere . . . . } Graf von Redern.
   c. Chor der Rachegeister . . . .

5. Ouverture zur Tragödie: „Struensee" . . . . Meyerbeer.
6. Terzett aus der Russischen Oper: „Das Leben für den Czar", gesungen von Frau *Herrenburger-Tuczeck*, Fräulein *Wagner* und Herrn *Mantius* . . . . . Glinka.
7. Fantasie für Pianoforte von *Arthur Napoleon* . . . . Thalberg.
8. Arie, gesungen von Fräulein *Wagner* . . . . Rossini.
9. Terzett, gesungen von Frau *Herrenburger-Tuczeck*, Fräulein *Wagner* und *Trietsch* . . . . Rossini.

Program of the concert on January 21st, 1857 in the White Hall of the Royal Palace in Berlin where the Trio from the opera "Ivan Susanin" ("Life for the Tsar") was performed.

On January 9, 1857 L. Herrenburger-Fouchek, J. Wagner and E. Mantius sang the trio in the White Hall of the Royal palace which was illuminated and glittering with precious stones. Glinka was satisfied with their performance and hurried to break this "pleasant news" to his sister.

It was to be Glinka's last letter. He caught a cold when he went out of the warm halls of the Royal palace into the frosty air. The flu aggravated his liver illness. At first, it did not worry the doctors. But on February 2/14 Doctor Bousse declared that Glinka's life was in danger. On the following day February 3/15 at 5 a.m. Glinka died "calmly, without evident signs of suffering" — V.N. Kashperov wrote to I.S. Turgenev on February 25/March 9, 1857. A post-mortem examination showed the death was due to steatosis of the liver.

On the morning of February 6 Glinka was buried in Troitskoye graveyard, not far from the grave of F. Mendelssohn-Bartholdy. Few came to say goodbye to him. Among them were Meyerbeer, Dehn, conductor Beier, V.N. Kashperov and one of the consuls of the Russian Embassy. In May of the same year the body of the great composer was taken by ship to Petersburg. It became possible due to Ludmila Ivanovna who overcame numerous obstacles in her path. On May 24, 1857 the body was committed to the earth in the cemetery of Alexander Nevsky Monastery.

The house in Französischestrasse 8, in Berlin where Glinka spent the last months of his life and where he died.

The news of Glinka's death made a painful impression on the music world of Petersburg. On February 23 a funeral service was performed in Konushennaya church, where twenty years before a funeral service had been performed over the body of Pushkin. On March 8 the Philharmonic Society gave a concert of Glinka's compositions; Glinka had been an honorary member of the Society. Glinka's friends and acquaintances took part in this concert, among them: D.M. Leonova, S.S. Artemovsky with K. Schubert conducting. The bust of the composer was erected on the scene.

Almost all Petersburg and Moscow newspapers and magazines responded to his death. "The New Poet", I.I. Panaev, found heartfelt words to commemorate Glinka's death in *Sovremennik:* ..."The name of Glinka has reached the most distant parts of Russia together with his melodious pensive or passionate sounds... Glinka's death is the greatest loss for the Russian musical world."

The last letter of Mikhail Glinka to his sister Ludmila Shestakova written on January 15/27, 1857 from Berlin.

Graves of Mikhail Glinka and his sister Ludmila Shestakova in the Leningrad (former Petersburg) Necropolis.

Chapter 6
IMMORTALITY

Glinka could have said about himself like Pushkin: "The news about me will cover all great Russia". However his compositions won recognition not only in Russia but all over the world. His gradual, consistent and insistent way of winning such recognition was not easy. It was hard to overcome hostility, condescending disregard and indifference to the creative work of the Russian composer as well as to the very fact of the existence of Russian music. The genius of Glinka, the founder of Russian classical music, overcame all obstacles. It made all admit the great value of Russian musical art for the culture of the world.

Russian music based on the realistic principles of Glinka's artistic ideas, has not won only universal acclaim but also greatly influenced other peoples' music development.

Mikhail Glinka's sister Ludmila Shestakova, the composer's most faithful and trustworthy friend, his heiress and promoter of his works, in the last years of her life.

Valse-Fantasie (the edition of 1856). The first page of the score with Glinka's own markings. He edited this piece several times. First dedicated to the "lady of his heart," Ekaterina Kern; in later years it was dedicated to Glinka's old-time friend K. Bulgakov.

Program of the concert of M. Glinka's composition conducted by G. von Bulov, Glasgow on December 29, 1877.

POPULAR

PART I

OVERTURE to the Tragedy "STRUENSEE"

(a) POLONAISE,
(b) WALTZ, } from "The Life for the Czar"
(c) KRAKOWIAK, }

RUSSIAN SONGS.

(a) Romance
(b) Romance

MDLLE. MARY LIDO.
(ACCOMPANIED ON THE PIANOFORTE BY MR. CHANNON CORNWALL)

(a) "KAMARINSKAJA," Scherzo,
(b) "A SUMMER NIGHT AT MADRID," Capriccio,

ROMANCE, "Sombres forêts," from "William Tell"

MDLLE. MARY LIDO.

OVERTURE to Sir Walter Scott's "MARMION"

INTERVAL OF TEN MINUTES.

Program of the concert of M. Glinka's compositions conducted by Johann Strauss in the Pavlovsk railway station on May 20, 1862.

All this became possible thanks to the noble efforts of many people. Some of them close to Glinka himself carefully collected and kept his music autographs, letters and insisted on including his compositions in the repertoire of the theatres and in concert programs. Glinka's sister and devoted friend Ludmila Ivanovna Shestakova was the first among them. The heiress of all of Glinka's fortune, she lived only for her "brother's music" and devoted her life to publicizing his music and immortalizing his name. The monuments to Glinka in Smolensk in 1886 and in Petersburg in 1906 were unveiled at her initiative and with her help. She died several months before the unveiling of the latter.

The activity of Glinka's devoted friend Vasily Pavlovitch Engelhardt is of paramount importance too. He energetically looked for and collected the manuscripts of the great composer. He presented his valuable collection to the manuscript department of the Petersburg Public Library, now the State Public Library named after M.E. Saltikov-Schedrin in Leningrad. Stasov was a very active collector of Glinka's autographs.

Johann Strauss, an Austrian composer and conductor devoted to Glinka's compositions, dedicated a special concert to his memory which took place at Pavlovsk station near Petersburg on May 20, 1862. Glinka's symphonic compositions were more and more often performed in the capital and concerts in the provinces followed. His music found its appropriate place in the concert programs of the Russian Music Society, the Free Music School directed by M.A. Balakirev and N.A. Rimsky-Korsakov, later by S.M. Liapunov, did very much to promote the works by the great composer. His works were in the programs of the Russian symphony concerts organized by M.P. Belaiev (Belaiev Concerts) in 1885. Prizes named after Glinka were also instituted. They are annually awarded to Russian composers for the best composition.

The initial plan of the opera "Ruslan and Ludmila" written in Pushkin's hand.

First edition of "Ruslan and Ludmila" by A.S. Pushkin, 1820.

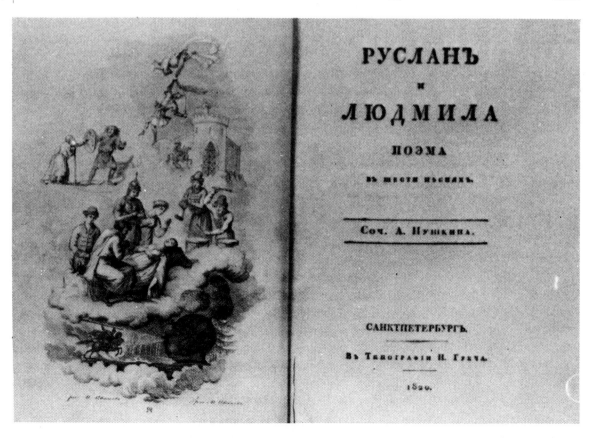

Glinka's music continued to win its recognition abroad too. His compositions were applauded in Brussels, Berlin and Glasgow. N.A. Rimsky-Korsakov opened the first Russian Symphony concert at the Paris World Exhibition on June 10, 1889 with the overture to *Ruslan and Ludmila*.

N.A. Rimsky-Korsakov and A.K. Liadov, under the guidance of M.A. Balakirev, prepared the scores of both operas by Glinka for publication in 1877-1881. "My admiration and worship of his genius were unlimited. Everything is so delicate and sometimes simple and natural", Rimsky-Korsakov wrote in *The Chronicle of My Musical Life* after the issue of Glinka's operas won world fame during the second half of the 19th and in the 20th centuries, especially after the Great October Revolution.

On February 21, 1939, in Moscow, in the Bolshoi Theatre the performance of Glinka's first opera was held. It was renewed under its original name *Ivan Susanin* with the new text of Soviet poet S.M. Gorodetsky; conductor — S.A. Samosud; set designer — P.V. Williams. On June 19 of the same year the opera was performed in Leningrad in the Opera Theatre named after S.M. Kirov, and in February 1940 in Odessa. In the following years it was performed in the majority of opera theatres of the USSR.

Now both operas by Glinka are always in the repertoires of the opera theatres of the U.S.S.R.

Scene from the first act of the opera "Ruslan and Ludmila" in the Berlin Opera House in the 1950's.

Sketch of the scenery to the second act of "Ruslan and Ludmila" made by the famous Russian painter K. Korovin, the Bolshoi Theatre, 1907.

Sketches of costumes for Finn, Ratmir and Chernomor by A. Golovin for the opera "Ruslan and Ludmila."

Alexander Vedernikov, soloist of the Bolshoi Theatre, as Ivan Susanin in the opera of the same name.

Evgeny Nesterenko, soloist of the Bolshoi Theatre, as Ruslan in the opera "Ruslan and Ludmila."

Great Russian singer Feodor Chaliapin (1873-1938) as Ivan Susanin. Drawing by a famous Russian painter I. Yershov.

Scene from the first act of the opera "Ivan Susanin" in the Prague National Theatre named after B. Smetana, 1949.

Sketches of costumes for the opera "Ivan Susanin" by V. Fedorovsky in the Leningrad Opera Theatre, 1940.

Celebrated Russian singer Antonina Nezhlanova (1843-1950) as Antonida in the opera "Ivan Susanin."

New generations of musicians, conductors, singers, instrumentalists refer to the music of the great composer.

Glinka's operas were prepared and conducted by M.A. Balakirev in Prague for the first time: *Ruslan and Ludmila* — in 1860, and *Ivan Susanin* — in 1867. *Ivan Susanin* was a great success in Milan and Russian singer A.G. Menshikova was invited to act as Antonida seven years later in 1874. Then it was a success in Berlin and other cities. Bulgarian singer Boris Khristov and Italian singer Renata Scotto brilliantly acted as Susanin and Antonida in La Scala in 1959. Michail Popov was very good as Susanin in Bulgaria.

Nikolay Gedda, an outstanding Swedish tenor, known as one of the best interpreters of Russian music and music by Glinka in particular, sang the part of Sobinin abroad.

Today operas by Glinka take an appropriate place in the repertoires of many opera theatres in the world.

Boris Khristov and Renata Scotto as Susanin and Antonida at La Scala, Milan, in 1959.

GREAT INTERPRETERS OF GLINKA'S MUSIC

Conductor Viatcheslav Suk (1861-1933).

Great Russian composer, pianist, and conductor Sergei Rachmaninoff (1873-1943).

Conductor Edward Napravnik (1839-1916)

Feodor Stravinsky (1843-1902) as Farlaf in the opera "Ruslan and Ludmila."

Lidia Zviagina (1864-1943) as Vania in the opera "Ivan
Susanin."

Osip Petrov as Farlaf in the opera "Ruslan and Ludmila."

Ivan Melnikov (1834-1906) as Ruslan in the opera "Ruslan and Ludmila."

Elisaveta Lavrovskaya (1845-1919) as Ratmir in the opera "Ruslan and Ludmila."

Zara Dolukhanova, a celebrated Soviet singer.

Irina Arkhipova, soloist of the Bolshoi Theatre, world-
famous Soviet opera singer.

Evgeny Svetlanov, a prominent Soviet conductor.

Ceremonial meeting in the Bolshoi Theatre commemorating the centenary of Mikhail Glinka's death, Moscow, 1957.

The Soviet people celebrated the 150th anniversary of the great Russian composer's birthday in June, 1954.

On behalf of millions of the Soviet people, thankful words for the joy Glinka's work brought to people were spoken both at the ceremonial meeting in the Bolshoi Theatre and at Glinka's home in Novospasskoye. Composer Shostakovich, laying a wreath on Glinka's monument in Smolensk, spoke about his genius too.

The centenary of Glinka's death was marked in February 1957. Ceremonial meetings commemorating the memory of the great classical composer of Russian music took place in the Soviet Union and many other countries.

Many Russian and Soviet musicians and scholars have thoroughly studied Glinka's works, written his scientifically documented biography, prepared the publication of the complete collection of his works and literary heritage. They are: V.F. Odoyevsky, A.N. Serov, H.A. Laroche, academician B.V. Asafiev, V.M. Bogdanov-Berezovsky, V.A. Vasina-Grossman, S.L. Ginsburg, N.N. Zagorny, E.I. Kann-Novikova, V.A. Kiselev, A.S. Liapunova, M.S. Pekelis, V.V. Protopopov, N.V. Tumanina, B.S. Steinpress and many others.

His operatic, symphonic, chamber-instrumental, piano and literary works are republished again and again. Millions of records of the great composer's music are issued.

The opening of a renewed estate of M.I. Glinka in the village of Novospasskoye took place in June, 1982. The house and the park where the composer spent his early years were reconstructed according to the descriptions of his contemporaries.

Glinka's work in music, like Pushkin's in literature, combined the high moral nature of Russian national musical art and its majestic beauty within classically harmonious forms. Here are the reasons for the Soviet peoples' love of this great composer and their appreciation of his genius.

The renewed estate of Mikhail Glinka in the village of Novospasskoye, opened for visitors since 1982.

Mikhail Glinka's grand piano made by I. Tischner, now exhibited in the Leningrad State Museum of musical instruments.

Choir "Slavsya" ("Glory") from the epilogue of the opera "Ivan Susanin."

The Bolshoi Stone Theatre (1817-1835) in Petersburg. Drawing by B. Sadovnikov (1830s).

INDEX

Illustrations are indicated in **bold** type.

Monument to Mikhail Glinka in Theatre Square in Leningrad by R. Bakh (1906).